OVERCOMING JEALOUSY

In the Church & In Ministry

THE SILENT DESTROYER

Floydise Paquette

REJOICE
Essential Publishing

Overcoming Jealousy In the Church & In Ministry/Floydise Paquette

ISBN-13: 978-1-946756-79-4

Library of Congress Control Number: 2019916823

DEDICATION

This book is dedicated to the One who entrusted and gifted me with this great work. How great is the love of our God and Father in Heaven, who prepared good things for us beforehand. May the Kingdom of His dear Son, Jesus Christ, be advanced, and the Family of God be strengthened and united for His glory. It is a privilege and honor to be a partaker of His heavenly calling and His grace.

TABLE OF CONTENTS

AUTHOR'S ADDRESS

I am so glad that you have decided to take up this book.

You have made an intentional decision and step toward becoming free.

You have decided knowingly or unknowingly that you would allow God to develop your character to strengthen you and to destroy the work of the enemy in your life.

Most of us know the familiar Scripture verse of John 10:10 that the enemy comes to steal, kill and to destroy, but Jesus came that we may have life and life more abundantly.

This Scripture verse is always timely and is an amazing weapon against the devices of the enemy. It is tremendous at helping us to stay encouraged, despite what the enemy is doing, because we know what God has already done through His Son Jesus. With this Scripture, we wage a good warfare. With this Scripture, we tell the enemy, NO! – And we tell God, YES!

This book did not make it to you by chance; this book is before you today so that God can bring change into your life—but also restoration to the body of Christ at large.

The weight of jealousy is about to be thrown off and it will no longer easily entangle you again.

You will be free to run the race that God has set before you. How do I know this? If you are taking up the sword against that vile spirit of jealousy, I know you aren't going to stop there!

The fact that you have recognized something within you is not right and you didn't deny it, speaks volumes in itself. Instead, you have decided to be sober and vigilant.

I pray that your mind will be renewed as you read through this book and that you would carefully consider the revelation and truths presented. May your life be transformed by the power of God's Holy Spirit.

WHAT IS JEALOUSY?

Declaration: Now that I have the knowledge, I shall not perish or suffer loss, but I shall overcome and recover all!

Before we dive in to the heart of the matter, allow me to set the framework for you to prepare your heart and mind to receive all that has been poured out. A proper foundation is paramount for the shift taking place, which will usher us into the healing, restoration and blessings God has in store for us. Together we overcome!

JEALOUS

According to the Merriam-Webster dictionary, "jealous" is defined as:

✳ Hostile toward a rival or one believed to enjoy an advantage.[1]

✳ (Jealousy) is a jealous disposition, attitude, or feeling.[2]

According to Dictionary.com, "jealous" is defined as:

✳ Feeling resentment because of another's success, advantage, etc.[3]

According to Google.com, "jealous" is defined as:

✳ Feeling or showing envy of someone or their achievements and advantages.[4]

Let me highlight some key words from these definitions:

Hostile | Rival | Resentment | Envy

Simply because someone appears to be successful, seems to enjoy an advantage or has achievements, we become hostile, make people our rivals, harbor resentment and become envious.

Is it actually as bad as it sounds? Yes! And—it is high time we treat it as such.

Be mindful, this spirit can manifest itself through us in a myriad of ways: through our disposition (temperament, temper, outlook, mood, personality), attitude, emotions (the way we feel), heart, mind, thoughts, and behavior— dictating what we do and what we don't do.

JEALOUSY IS DANGEROUS

Proverbs 27:4 NLT
Anger is cruel, and wrath is like a flood,
    but jealousy is even more dangerous.

We have all seen, heard or experienced how destructive anger can be and there is no doubt that wrath is quite treacherous, but I imagine not many knew the bible said jealousy is even more dangerous than these.

From this moment on, I hope you will no longer take this lightly.

Jealousy is reckless! It is sneaky, deceitful and S I L E N T – that is until the damage is done and it is too late for any kind of reconstructive recourse.

Being jealous is a serious condition of the heart to which we can no longer close our eyes. Jealousy is also a spirit—it's demonic (James 3:15 NLT). When many of you hear this, it comes as no surprise or objection. Jealousy is also disorderly in nature? How is that, you may ask? Jealousy seeks to destroy you from the inside out. Anything that will cause you to become self-destructive is disorderly.

I have provided some practical scenarios, which will bring further understanding. This chapter and subsequent chapters will shed light using common examples from situations and circumstances that, undoubtedly, many have experienced.

James 3:16 NLT
For wherever there is jealousy and selfish ambition, there you will find disorder and evil of every kind.

2 Corinthians 12:20 NLT
For I am afraid that when I come I won't like what I find, and you won't like my response. I am afraid that I will find quarreling, jealousy, anger, selfishness, slander, gossip, arrogance, and disorderly behavior.

Upfront, let me ask you this: Have you ever told someone, "I hope you do well!"—wearing a huge smile on your face, while on the inside you really hoped they didn't?

You were saying one thing, but inside you felt completely differently. The sad truth is, you knew it, but they didn't. Yet, you proceeded to say and do things contrary to how you felt or what you wanted. What's worse is you wanted the other person to believe what you were saying or doing was true and coming from a good place—hence, the big smile. Yet the truth of the matter is—it came from a different spirit altogether and you were operating in deception.

1 Peter 2:1 NLT
So get rid of all evil behavior. Be done with all deceit, hypocrisy, jealousy, and all unkind speech.

Do you see what evil behavior jealousy is grouped with? Deceit, hypocrisy and all unkind speech. So, if you weren't certain if your jealous behavior was of a deceitful nature, I hope this has brought clarity.

This reminds me of the account in the Bible where the demon-possessed slave girl, walked daily behind Paul and some other believers, saying what sounded to be good and complimentary. Though it was the truth, it was coming from the wrong spirit.

Acts 16:17-18 NKJV:
[17] This girl followed Paul and us, and cried out, saying, "These men are the servants of the Most High God, who proclaim to us the way of salvation." [18] And this she did for many days.

But Paul, greatly annoyed, turned and said to the spirit, "I command you in the name of Jesus Christ to come out of her." And he came out that very hour.

It is my hope that just as Paul became greatly annoyed at this evil spirit, we too would become just as annoyed by this spirit of jealousy plaguing the church and begin to assert our authority over it.

However, we can't take authority over it before we recognize it. Recognition is key and acknowledgment is also just as important.

Ignorance and turning a blind eye are no longer options. We need to be able to recognize when this spirit is present and operating in ourselves and others. We must begin to come out of agreement, take authority and cast it out!

When you recognize it in others, it's not to call out, confront, condemn or cut people off. On the contrary, I would encourage you to pray for them—first. Ask God to convict them and bring them to repentance for salvation. Ask God to protect you, protect them and protect the relationship. Keep your heart pure and open to them.

As for yourself, don't tolerate jealousy! Be fervent in prayer and use your authority.

Let's dig in and look at some other biblical accounts where jealousy brought about destruction, adverse actions and consequences and see what we can glean from them.

Buckle your seatbelts! Indeed, you are about to be blessed and set free!

2

MANIFESTATIONS OF JEALOUSY

Declaration: No weapon formed against me shall prosper!

IT'S TIME TO PAY ATTENTION!

Let me remind you of what one of the definitions of jealousy is from the Merriam-Webster dictionary:

—Jealousy is a jealous <u>disposition</u>, <u>attitude</u>, or <u>feeling</u>.[2]

I want to point this out to you again here since we are on the subject of how jealousy tends to manifest itself in a wide variety of ways. I want you to be able to recognize when this spirit is manifesting itself in your life and in your relationships. Detection is key. Although for the most part, I believe many of us are able to recognize or detect when this spirit manifests, I also believe that many simply choose to ignore it. Out of those of us who do acknowledge it, few will intentionally come against it.

Today, this changes! We will recognize it, acknowledge it and take a vigilant stand to ensure this spirit no longer has power or influence over us.

Going forward you should more easily be able to recognize when your disposition, attitude or feelings shift in response to a manifestation of jealousy. It's not just a feeling—it's an attitude—it's a disposition. It is a tendency to "act" in a certain manner under the given circumstances.

We are going to keep an eye on our emotions, thoughts, behaviors, actions and responses and begin to bring our flesh under the subjection of Christ.

When you feel that twinge of agitation when someone else receives recognition or honor, gets addressed by someone of notable distinction (the apostle, prophet, pastor or teacher), is given a promotion, responsibility, title, spotlight, microphone, platform, praise, accolades, compliments, comments, shares, buzz, and gets noticed by leaders or people of prominence—don't just ignore the manifestation! Check it, rebuke it, and command that spirit to leave. Go to God in prayer and see if there are any roots that you need to address. Ask Him to help you and to cleanse you of anything that will hinder you from walking in love with Him and others.

T.R.I.B.E.

Are you feeling or have ever felt left out or left behind? At times, do you struggle to know where you fit in? Have you been wondering, "Is this the right group, the right place, the right people or the right time for me?"

I want you to be prayerful, so that you will know your T.R.I.B.E.—Team, Responsibilities, Involvement, Boundaries, and the Expected End. Know who you are supposed to be connected to, how, why and when (the timing). Is the connection for a reason, a season or a long-term commitment? If it's for a reason or work, complete the work God joined you together to accomplish and then release each other to continue walking on your respective journeys with the Lord. I'm not saying you have to cut all ties. I'm saying make sure you don't hold on to people and cause them to miss assignments God chose them to do because they're trying to be faithful or loyal to you and vice versa. If it's for a season, it is imperative that you know your seasons and the timing of God. Don't put people in the wrong category. Don't abuse their role in your life and don't over-step the boundaries of your role in their lives.

If you don't understand the purpose for which a person was sent into your life, you risk destroying the good fruit intended to be produced from the relationship, due to misplaced and inappropriate expectations. Frustration can set in, ultimately leading to a premature ending of the relationship.

In order to safeguard our relationships, we have to be willing to recognize where we err in our ways, be willing to grow and make adjustments.

MANIFESTATIONS

Here's a list of some of the many manifestations of jealousy you may notice that we'll touch on in more detail individually. I feel it is necessary to put them in list form before diving in.

o Feeling Insignificant
o Feeling Overlooked
o Feeling Left Out
o Comparison
o Competition
o Covetousness
o Strife, Contention, Division, Drama
o Anger
o Envy
o Miscommunication

o Sabotage & Destruction
o Accusation & Blame
o Slander
o Defensive
o Derision
o Easily Offended
o Infatuation & Obsessive Thoughts
o Insults
o Control
o The Disqualifier

o Hoping Someone Fails   o Attention, Attention

o Hoping Someone Stops o The Critic

✳ Feeling Insignificant

You would be surprised at the number of people who are plagued with a feeling of insignificance. One of our core needs is to feel as though we actually make a difference. No one wants to "just be there." We don't want to feel like we're there, but not really needed or necessary. We want our inclusion to be valuable and what we do to be impactful. As many of us may have experienced, it can be quite unsettling to be amongst people who are great, yet we "feel" insignificant.

This is one of those inner battles that no one else knows you're fighting. We show up with a smile and when people ask how we are doing, we say all is well. Yet no one knows you are struggling with your self-esteem. Sometimes it can feel like you're the only one with a certain issue, while everyone else around you seem to be flourishing in that same area.

Insignificance is the main place where we tend to discount what we bring to the table and magnify the contributions of others. We can easily see where what "they" brought is necessary, but struggle with whether or not what we have is good enough.

I want you to come to the realization, even if it takes much prayer and coming before the Lord, what He gave you is more than enough. What we consider small is something God is waiting for you to show up with, so that He can use it for His glory. It may seem like "just oil," "just a smooth stone and a sling shot," "just a walk around a wall," "just a shout," "just a prayer," "just a song," or "just a word." However, if God gave it to you, it is JUST what it takes, JUST what is needed and very significant! You are very significant!

✳ Feeling Overlooked

In ideal situations and circumstances, it would be great to be considered, thought of, highly recommended, recognized, first choice, given a part, included, invited, accepted, embraced, welcomed, cared for—you get it. Sometimes, this is not the case and when it's not, those who already have a history with feelings of unworthiness, insignificance, rejection, etc., the manifestation of "feeling" overlooked can seem magnified.

I want the sons and daughters of God to receive the healing we need, so we don't continue to manifest all over the place.

In all sincerity and solemnity, it's really time to drop out of the "What about me?" stage play.

Have you noticed that whenever the "what about me" part comes to the stage, it brings with it other feelings that pull you down quick and deep? Feelings of frustration and irritation—you feel slighted, forgotten, abandoned, cast to the side, excluded, and discouraged. You feel like God is holding out on you, even though His Word tells us no good thing will He withhold from you—that is, from those who walk uprightly before Him—which I know is you. You start to blame yourself for everything you "might" have done that's getting in the way of what you want. Then, condemnation tries to wiggle in and before you know it, you've sank so low you need to be picked up and lifted out of a pit.

"What about me" has NEVER felt good and it never came with encouragement. Let's face it, it makes you feel downright miserable. Even if you feel propelled to do something great from the position of "what about me," it's likely not from a pure place of God's love for you. So yes, break up with "what about me," and cast it down knowing that God is for you and not against you. He wants to do great things with you, in you and for you.

Philippians 1:15 NLT
It's true that some are preaching out of jealousy and rivalry. But others preach about Christ with pure motives.

Ecclesiastes 4:4 NLT

Then I observed that most people are motivated to success because they envy their neighbors. But this, too, is meaningless—like chasing the wind.

God does not overlook any one of us. Your purpose and destiny are indisputable. He makes sure they are fulfilled and come to pass. He completes the good work He began in us. Make sure when you come forth, you come forth with a pure heart, motivated by the love of God.

✳ Feeling Left Out

Why is it that when we see a group of women, who we never personally desired to hang out with, come together for a special purpose, outing, project or fellowship, all of a sudden, we feel left out? You see them having a good time or accomplishing great things and you start to feel like you're missing out and now have a desire to belong and to be a part.

The dynamics of a group are sometimes simple, but they can get complicated, delicate, misunderstood or difficult to explain because oftentimes, there is an unspoken bond that holds the group together. This unspoken bond can sometimes create the appearance of a clique during times when everyone should be welcome. In these instances, you feel like certain others are accepted, preferred or valued; yet, you weren't chosen, invited or even considered.

❋ Comparison

Galatians 6:4 NLT
Pay careful attention to your own work, for then you will get the satisfaction of a job well done, and you won't need to compare yourself to anyone else.

I stand in total agreement with the Word of God and I urge you again, pay **careful attention** to your own work. As I've mentioned in this book, we have a crippling tendency to discount, despise and discredit our own work, experiences and blessings; while on the other hand, we magnify the work, experiences and blessings of others.

Pay careful attention to what God is doing in your life. Pay careful attention to how He is blessing you. Pay careful attention to what He is producing in you and through you. Be intentional about looking for all of the good. Recall how God has blessed you, kept you, delivered you, saved you, healed you, rescued you and made Himself known to you. Give Him thanks!

Don't cheat yourself. Get the satisfaction of a job well done. Think about all the times God has blessed the work of your hands. Think about all the times He made the work of your hands prosper. There were many times that various things worked out so great you knew it had to be the Lord who was on your side. There were so many times where everything seemed to come together and everything fell into place. There were many times when you know you messed up, fell short, didn't give it all you had, but God still came through and caused everything to work together for your good.

It's worth repeating: If you pay careful attention to your own work, then you will get the satisfaction of a job well done, and you won't need to compare yourself to anyone else. When you're dissatisfied with your own work, you start looking over into the lives of others. Commonly, one of two things will happen: you would either come out looking better or come out looking worse, both of which are false estimations based on unjust scales.

The very purpose of comparison has always been to determine which or who is better. This may work well in the world as we compare cars, houses, professions, schools, etc. to determine which will better suit our needs; however, comparing ourselves one to another does not work well in the Kingdom of God. There is no Godly edification, comfort or encouragement in determining you're better or that someone else is better than you. This type of behavior is destructive and no good thing can come from it.

✳ Competition

Needless to say, this is one of the main weapons the enemy uses against us with the spirit of jealousy. Let me say, it is very unfortunate that it has been so effective. Good news—it no longer has to be! It's easy to say, "I don't have to be in competition with her," but they are merely words if we don't deal with the root of the issue. You can absolutely hate competing with someone, but the truth is, if you are not healed and restored, you will find yourself competing. You will find yourself doing the very thing you do not want to do. Your spirit is willing, but your flesh is weak.

According to the Merriam-Webster dictionary, the definition of compete is:

- to strive consciously or unconsciously for an objective (such as position, profit, or a prize)
- be in a state of rivalry.[5]

There is a striving in the church and we have set ourselves one against another, both consciously and unconsciously for a position, a profit or a prize. We have not fully considered and understood that we do not have to compete for anything God has already given us. We are lacking in our understanding that our work was established before the foundation of the earth and it was hidden in Christ Jesus. Who can thwart the plans of the Lord? Before you were in your mother's womb, He knew you and His plans for you are certain. There is an expected end for you. Why are we fighting for what is already ours? We are wrestling against flesh and blood, against each other in the Kingdom of Heaven. Has God set us against each other? From what I read, He turned an army against itself in confusion and they killed each other with their swords (1 Samuel 14). Was it the army of God? No— it was the army of our real enemy.

Come out of agreement with competition so that we don't continue to suffer the destruction for which our enemies were destined.

Galatians 5:15-16 NLT

[15] But if you are always biting and devouring one another, watch out! Beware of destroying one another. [16] So I say, let the Holy Spirit guide your lives. Then you won't be doing what your sinful nature craves.

Are you ready for the victory that is before the army of God? It will take our fighting together against our enemies, not against each other.

✳ Covetousness

I like the way Merriam Webster defines the term covetous. The following is the definition provided for those who are learning the English language. As such, it was intended to be simple and easy to understand:

- 'Feeling or showing a very strong desire for something that you do not have and especially for something that belongs to someone else'[6]

Covetousness is age-old and typical worldly behavior. We often see this behavior present in children—as soon as they see you with something, not only do they desire it, but they want to take it. Those who are selfish would rather no one has what they desire, if they themselves can't have it. But as the bible exhorts us:

1 Corinthians 13:11 NLT
When I was a child, I spoke and thought and reasoned as a child. But when I grew up, I put away childish things.

Such behavior, speech, thinking and reasoning is not fit for the Kingdom.

Many in the body of Christ have coveted the blessings of others, what God has done for them, their gifts and callings, their part in the body, their assignments, their influence, their reputation, their success and even their "appearance" of success.

We already know without saying, not everyone is called to the nations. Not everyone will have a congregation of ten thousand, not everyone will have a social media following of one hundred thousand, not everyone will be a doctor or a lawyer and yes, not everyone is an apostle, a prophet, a teacher, a worker of miracles, or have gifts of healing (1 Corinthians 12:29-30).

1 Corinthians 12:22-27 NKJV

[22]No, much rather, those members of the body which seem to be weaker are necessary. [23] And those members of the body which we think to be less honorable, on these we bestow greater honor; and our unpresentable parts have greater modesty, [24] but our presentable parts have no need. But God composed the body, having given greater honor to that part which lacks it, [25] that there should be no schism in the body, but that the members should have the same care for one another. [26] And if one member suffers, all the members suffer with it; or if one member is honored, all the members rejoice with it. [27] Now you are the body of Christ, and members individually.

Not everybody is called to walk in the same level or degree of visibility. Too many are vying for the stage, the lime-light, and the microphone and are thereby neglecting the work to which they are called.

I urge you to seek God about your part in the body of Christ and the works He graciously prepared for you in Christ Jesus before the foundation of the world for you to walk in "them," not to covet someone else's part. Be careful about covetousness. When you stand before God to give an account for what you did with the talents He gave you, you can't say you were busy chasing after something else. Make your calling and election sure and run your race well.

Let us be comfortable with where we are placed in the body and let us encourage those who may not be as visible and show them the same care as we would show those who are more visible.

I want you to pay close attention to verses 22 and 23. I want you to let it sink deep down into your heart— YOU ARE NECESSARY AND HAVE BEEN GIVEN GREAT HONOR.

I also think verse 27 is paramount because God is reminding us that not only are we a part of the body at large, but as members INDIVIDUALLY, YOU matter. You are unique and vital.

Here are some examples I can give for those who may not be as visible but extremely important and totally deserving of great honor: those who often retreat into their rooms, closing the door behind them, and praying to God in secret; and those who labor in prayer on behalf of their families, the church, our nations, etc., when no one is watching or listening. What about those who offer administrative help and keep the church and ministries going? Yes, those who give financially; those who show mercy and kindness to those around them without needing a title or a position. How honorable!

There is a saying: Bloom where you are planted! Let your light so shine that men would see your good works and glorify your Father in Heaven! Hallelujah! God has given us all the potential, the power, the willingness and the ability to do what is pleasing to Him.

Covet no more, for the treasure that God has put on the inside of YOU is needed to manifest in the earth. You can never present to Him what He has given to someone else.

✳ Strife, contention, division, drama!

James 4:1-3 NLT

What is causing the quarrels and fights among you? Don't they come from the evil desires at war within you? [2] You want what you don't have, so you scheme and kill to get it. You are jealous of what others have, but you can't get it, so you fight and wage war to take it away from them. Yet you don't have what you want because you don't ask God for it. [3] And even when you ask, you don't get it because your motives are all wrong—you want only what will give you pleasure.

This is an interesting manifestation that shows itself in a myriad of ways. The most common manifestations are quarreling, disagreements and arguments. Oftentimes, when you are jealous, you are easily frustrated by the person of whom you're jealous. Do you find yourself getting downright irked by everything a "certain" person says or does?

Galatians 5:19-21 NLT

[19] When you follow the desires of your sinful nature, the results are very clear: sexual immorality, impurity, lustful pleasures, [20] idolatry, sorcery, hostility, quarreling, jealousy, outbursts of anger, selfish ambition, dissension, division, [21] envy, drunkenness, wild parties, and other sins like these. Let me tell you again, as I have before, that anyone living that sort of life will not inherit the Kingdom of God.

Strife is an earnest endeavor to create conflict. We should be earnest about many things and the bible names a few, but conflict, contention and division are not some of them.

Let's face it, the drama in the church has to cease. The church and the people of God are supposed to be places of refuge and safety. If you want to get away from drama, you should be able to find peace in the church.

If you've found yourself being argumentative, the one who just doesn't want to agree, the one who is just plain bothered, take a step back and evaluate your heart, your error and where your earnestness has been. If you've not been earnestly praying, seeking after God for Him and His way, desiring the most "helpful" gifts so that you can be of help and not a hindrance, now is the time to make it right.

1 Corinthians 3:3 NLT

for you are still controlled by your sinful nature. You are jealous of one another and quarrel with each other. Doesn't that prove you are controlled by your sinful nature? Aren't you living like people of the world?

✳ Anger

We've read in the beginning Proverbs 27:4 that says anger is cruel. Did you ever consider that—anger being "cruel?" It is cruel for us to act out in anger. What good has ever come from an outburst of anger? What good conclusion was ever drawn out of anger? From anger comes murder, payback, vengeance, cursing, violence, etc. Have you ever burned with anger? You can literally and physically feel yourself getting really hot. Am I right? Your palms and your head even start to sweat from the burning taking place from within. This is dangerous and self-destructive.

This is why the bible admonishes us to be slow to anger. You think the other person is about to get it, but you have no idea the consequences that ends up being dumped on your own head. Do you remember when Haman got angry because Mordecai wouldn't bow down to him? He planned Mordecai's destruction, but he ended up trapped by his own wiles.

Anger is an enemy to a sound mind.

Psalm 4:4 NLT
Don't sin by letting anger control you.
    Think about it overnight and remain silent.

✳ Envy

Envy is synonymous to jealousy. Both leave you feeling discontented or resentful. Both leave you desiring and wanting to have something you see someone else with.

I really thought Wikipedia's definition was quite interesting:

Envy is an emotion which "occurs when a person lacks another's superior quality, achievement, or possession and either desires it or wishes that the other lacked it."[7]

I think the latter part of the definition says a mouthful. If we don't have it, we don't want to see the person we're jealous of with it either. How sad that we would actually wish the other person lacked the very thing we ourselves want. It is so twisted.

I don't know much about Aristotle and my goal is not to point to him in any way, but Wikipedia quotes him in its definition of envy. He defined it as "pain at the sight of another's good fortune."[7] How troubling. This is just another way to sum up the point regarding envy. This definition is an accurate and noteworthy mention.

Someone else's prosperity should not cause us pain. It should not be painful to witness nor painful to hear about. On the contrary, it should give us hope and cause us to rejoice and give God glory.

It's really time to be sober and vigilant against the spirits of jealousy and envy.

✳ Miscommunication

When you are dealing with a spirit of jealousy, oftentimes, what you hear gets filtered through that spirit. The things people say become jaded, twisted and taken out of context.

When your hearing is muddied by the unclean spirit of jealousy, the way you receive things that are done or spoken often confirms the agenda of the enemy and not the truth. Be careful!

---

*You become guarded for the wrong reasons
and vigilant without a true cause.*

"Yup, she thinks she's better than me!" Have you ever said or thought this to yourself? Take note, that may not be the truth, it just might be jealousy.

How often do those around you have to end up saying, "I didn't mean it that way." Well, maybe they didn't—maybe it's really not them, but it's you!

✳ Hoping Someone Fails

I know—this is a hard pill to swallow, so let me put it differently. You are quick to say, "Good luck," "God bless you," "I hope all goes well," "I pray you succeed and prosper," "I pray God uses you mightily," etc., all the while, as you speak these words, you feel something on the contrary stirring deep on the inside. You begin to feel very uncomfortable at the thought that they just might kill it, they just might prosper and then...where would that leave you? How are you going to measure up to that? Well, let me take off some of the pressure—YOU DON'T MEASURE UP TO THAT! They are not your barometer!

Depending on where you are in your walk with God and your level of maturity, you may either ignore these thoughts of hoping someone fails, entertain them, let them fester and build, or repent. You may ask God to forgive you, pull down the negative thoughts and cleanse you of all of that jealous unrighteousness.

I know—you're not a total monster and you're not a bad person. The truth is, you really do love/like the other person.

Let's face it, it can be downright upsetting to have these feelings going on inside of you. I know I hated them. It was extremely bothersome to have such thoughts and feelings that I knew were absolutely displeasing to God. It didn't feel good or right to have these feelings. So let me tell you, I prayed for God to help me and to deliver me.

Romans 12:15 NLT
Be happy with those who are happy, and weep with those who weep.

Jealousy will cause you to do the opposite. Don't treat this lightly because others may not see it. Don't treat it lightly because it happens in your heart, where it is seemingly hidden and unnoticed. You may not laugh out loud when someone else is weeping, hurting or in distress, but your heart responds with subtle satisfaction.

There is a false peace and a false rest that communicates it is now safe to let down your guard because that person is no longer a threat to you in their distress, in their brokenness, or in their failure, so now you can relax.

Oh, how wicked it is for our hearts to rejoice, even ever so slightly, when our brothers and sisters are weeping. Heart check!

How many of us have consoled or comforted ourselves with the wickedness in our hearts?

Genesis 27:38, 41-42 NKJV

38 And Esau said to his father, "Have you only one blessing, my father? Bless me—me also, O my father!" And Esau lifted up his voice and wept.

41 So Esau hated Jacob because of the blessing with which his father blessed him, and Esau said in his heart, "The days of mourning for my father are at hand; then I will kill my brother Jacob."

42 And the words of Esau her older son were told to Rebekah. So she sent and called Jacob her younger son, and said to him, "Surely your brother Esau **comforts himself concerning you by intending to kill you.**

First, I want to give thanks to the Lord, our God, for the truth that He doesn't have only one blessing. He is absolutely delighted to bless every one of us. So, we don't have to weep in bitterness over the blessings that He gives to our brothers and sisters. We don't have to inwardly hope they fail, stumble or mess up.

Now, you may read this account about Esau and think, "Well, I'm not trying to kill anybody." Let me tell you this: you may not be trying to kill anyone physically, but let us remember what the bible says about jealousy:

Proverbs 27:4 NLT
Anger is cruel, and wrath is like a flood,
    but jealousy is even more dangerous.

If jealousy is more dangerous than anger and wrath, be careful and guard your heart. While you may not commit physical murder, you are not likely going to get behind your brother or sister in Christ and push them toward success as they do their part to advance the Kingdom of Heaven. God put it plainly, he who is not with me is against me. One heart-felt, fervent prayer on their behalf has the power to catapult them and strengthen them, but will you make this petition on their behalf or will you remain silent, ignoring both the jealousy and the opportunity to support them?

Genesis 4:8 NLT

One day Cain suggested to his brother, "Let's go out into the fields." And while they were in the field, Cain attacked his brother, Abel, and killed him.

Be careful! Jealousy can cause you to try to lead people somewhere to their demise or their destruction. It can cause you to attempt to lead people to places that are not good for them, to places that are dry and they can't flourish, to places which God has not called or sent them. Jealousy will cause you to attempt to uproot people.

To Whose Credit?

Let us consider the crazy relationship between Saul and David. Jealousy is so convoluted that you can be benefiting from the anointing of God on someone's life and still try to kill them or shut them down. Saul was greatly tormented by an evil spirit and even while David ministered to him, Saul tried to kill him. How often have we tried to bite the hand that feeds us in our family, in our church, in the workplace, or in ministry? We know some of the greatest hurt have come from those we poured into, gave the clothes off our backs and for whom we've labored in love. Oftentimes, you may have asked, "...and this is how they repay me?"

How many times have you mistreated the very person or persons who have helped you the most, who have tried to befriend you or support you? Yet, it was difficult to receive from them and stand with them because you were jealous of their anointing?

1 Samuel 18:8-9 NLT

[8] This made Saul very angry. "What's this?" he said. "They credit David with ten thousands and me with only thousands. Next they'll be making him their king!" [9] So from that time on Saul kept a jealous eye on David.

It was the very next day after Saul said this and became jealous that he was tormented again by an evil spirit and again needed David's help. He used this as an opportunity to attempt to take his life. This is a great example that no matter how we feel about a person, if God has anointed them and is with them, it would be in your best interest not to set yourself against them. Yes...not even in your heart.

Saul was totally thrown off by what was credited to David and what was credited to him. I would gracefully admonish leaders (or anyone else) to be careful in this regard, as some may feel they should be "credited" more than those they lead or oversee, because of their title or position.

We are now, in the body of Christ, recognizing and saying with our mouths that as leaders, we want those who follow after us to produce more, to produce double, etc. Be careful that you don't just say this with your mouth, but not have this hope in your heart. Between you and God, you have to be humble and honest so that you can get the help you need. Ask yourself, is there any jealousy in me?

It is just as critical for us all to be sober. How often are we calculating and keeping track of what others are being credited? The bible says that from that time on Saul kept a "jealous" eye on David.

Have the eyes which have seen the victories of others become "jealous" eyes? Be careful—if your eyes, which are the light of your body is dark, how great is that darkness?

Matthew 6:22-23 NKJV
[22] "The lamp of the body is the eye. If therefore your eye is good, your whole body will be full of light. [23] But if your eye is bad, your whole body will be full of darkness. If therefore the light that is in you is darkness, how great is that darkness!

Mark 7:21-23 NLT
[21] For from within, out of a person's heart, come evil thoughts, sexual immorality, theft, murder, [22] adultery, greed, wickedness, deceit, lustful desires, envy, slander, pride, and foolishness. [23] All these vile things come from within; they are what defile you."

✳ Hoping Someone Stops

"Stop, just stop, STOP!" Have you ever screamed this to yourself on the inside? Perhaps while someone was in the middle of an exemplary performance, ministering under the power and anointing of God, or praying like a warrior, etc.?

All the while, you sit there...

Feigning joy over their accomplishments, while inside you're manifesting!

✳ Sabotage & Destruction

We know clearly that the enemy comes to steal, kill and destroy. As believers we don't tear down the work of other believers, we tear down and destroy the works of the devil. However, at times, the enemy is success-ful in his schemes, even if temporarily, to sabotage the work of God's sent ones. Unfortunately, it is with the help of our brothers and sisters in Christ. We are oftentimes, unaware of when we are partnering with the agenda of the enemy because it looks and feels like, "we just don't agree" with what our brothers and sisters are doing. As such, we feel justified in not supporting and making sure no one else comes along to support either.

Acts 5:17-18 NLT

[17] The high priest and his officials, who were Sadducees, were filled with jealousy. [18] They arrested the apostles and put them in the public jail.

Jealousy will cause you to go against the very work of God. The Apostles were working miracles, healing the sick and those possessed by evil spirits. All the while, the high priest and his officials, who were Sadducees, were filled with jealousy. Jealousy wants to arrest your spirit and shut you down. Jealousy wants to sabotage and destroy what looks like accomplishment and great feats.

Sabotage will bring slander, disruption, damage, interruption and interference.

Be careful of what you whole-heartedly fight against if you have not prayed to God to find out what He is doing and who He is using. If God has not given you the assignment to tear down, be very careful. It would behoove some of us to follow after Gamaliel's sound advice found later in the account:

Acts 5:38-39

[38] "So my advice is, leave these men alone. Let them go. If they are planning and doing these things merely on their own, it will soon be overthrown. [39] But if it is from God, you will not be able to overthrow them. You may even find yourselves fighting against God!"

Let's keep our hands and our mouths to ourselves, unless we are sent by God to do otherwise. Don't be hasty and in the end find yourself in error; seek first the Lord.

WILL YOU STAND OR MAKE A SHUT DOWN ATTEMPT?

Genesis 26:12-16 NLT

[12] When Isaac planted his crops that year, he harvested a hundred times more grain than he planted, for the LORD blessed him. [13] He became a very rich man, and his wealth continued to grow. [14] He acquired so many flocks of sheep and goats, herds of cattle, and servants that the Philistines became jealous of him. [15] So the Philistines filled up all of Isaac's wells with dirt. These were the wells that had been dug by the servants of his father, Abraham.

[16] Finally, Abimelech ordered Isaac to leave the country. "Go somewhere else," he said, "for you have become too powerful for us."

We have to be able to stand when God blesses other people. Not only do we want to shut people down or shut them up, but we also want them to leave! The Philistines told Isaac he became too powerful. One thing we know is, it becomes very uncomfortable when people with a grasshopper mentality identifies another person as a giant. Insecurity, inferiority and intimidation threaten those who feel like the power of a giant causes them to be insignificant.

People with a grasshopper mentality don't want to occupy the same space with a giant.

Sadly, there are many who felt or experienced jealousy in the church or amongst their brothers and sisters in the body of Christ and were forced out or felt they had no other choice but to leave. People didn't want to make room for their gifts, their anointing, or their purpose. Whether we've experienced the grasshopper, the giant or both, it's time to be sanctified by the truth, healed, and delivered. It's time to begin walking as sons and daughters who are led by the Spirit of God, in the unity of the faith, and measuring up to the full stature of Christ.

BE DISCERNING & GET OUT OF THE WAY

1 Corinthians 12:8-11 KJV

[8] For to one is given by the Spirit the word of wisdom; to another the word of knowledge by the same Spirit;

[9] To another faith by the same Spirit; to another the gifts of healing by the same Spirit;

[10] To another the working of miracles; to another prophecy; to another discerning of spirits; to another divers kinds of tongues; to another the interpretation of tongues:

¹¹ But all these worketh that one and the selfsame Spirit, dividing to every man severally as he will.

We must learn how to not only partner with God but unite and partner with what God is doing through others. We must honor the work of the Holy Spirit as He manifests Himself as He wills in a diversity of ways, in a diversity of people. We must be careful not to quench or oppose the Holy Spirit as He moves. You may think you're just hindering the person in the moment, only to find out you were actually fighting against the Holy Spirit.

Ananias and Sapphira thought they were lying to Peter, but Peter made it clear they were lying to the Holy Spirit (Acts 5:3-4). It cost them their lives. We have to be very discerning in this hour. When God is working and using His sons and daughters as vessels, partner, participate, cooperate, make room, and let the Spirit of the living God have His way.

It's not about you. It's about the Kingdom. It's about the will of God. It's a good time to humble yourself and not think more highly of yourself than you ought. It's a good time to esteem others as higher than yourself. It's a good time to not demand your own way. Gone are the days of the one-man shows. If God wanted just one man, Jesus would've been sufficient. But He trained "us" as His disciples, gave us His Spirit and sent us just as He was sent. Jesus said that it was good for us that He leaves.

When the Holy Spirit came, He didn't just come to a select ten of the 120 in the upper room. He came to the 120! It is God's good pleasure to pour out His Spirit on all flesh—not so that we can boast as if we've done anything, but so that His will and the work He prepared for us can be accomplished. Get out of the way and let the light in others shine!

YOU HAVE YOUR OWN WORK TO DO!

Ephesians 2:10 NKJV

For we are His workmanship, created in Christ Jesus for good works, which God prepared beforehand that we should walk in them.

Let me encourage you brethren, there are works that God prepared for his people to walk in. In His Word, God tells us, concerning Jesus, He will ensure His purpose is fulfilled. We know based on Scripture no matter what the enemy tried to do, the will of God was going to be done. No matter what people tried to do, no matter who accepted Jesus or who rejected Him, the will of the Lord was going to be done.

How many of us are standing in the way of the work of the Lord that He has prepared long before we even entered the Earth, for others to walk in? How many of us are allowing jealousy to attempt to muzzle the mouths of those to whom God has given a word? How many of us, find it difficult to make room for the gifts of the Holy Spirit to flow in other people's lives? How many of us have shut out and rejected people simply because they were anointed and God was using them? How many of us today are standing in the way of the Lord or opposing his work and we think it's as simple as opposing the person?

✳ Accusation & Blame

Jealousy will make you think the other person has ulterior motives.

Don't let your mind become a carnival mirror for the spirit of jealousy. This spirit wants to bring distortion. It wants to grab hold of what you hear and see and twist it into unrecognizable forms of evil. It's a trick of the enemy. Don't be ignorant of his devices. Shatter the carnival mirror.

Jealousy will distort the truth and turn the person you are jealous of into a hideous monster. Recognize the moment this person becomes an enemy in your mind and shut down the spirit behind this lie. Jealousy will make a person your nemesis. It's a real battle and the enemy has your demise in mind. I urge you to pray for deliverance, for the destruction of your real enemy, praise the Lord and bless the person.

Accusation and blame will cause you to inwardly accuse people of having impure motives and selfish ambitions. You will question and become critical of everything they do.

Please don't exalt your gift of discernment. We have to intentionally and aggressively deal with this spirit of jealousy. We thank God for the gift, but right now we are addressing the spirit in operation that's not from God. This is not the time to use your anointing as a scapegoat or cover-up. It's time to deal with the jealousy hidden in your heart.

David prayed to God and asked, "Cleanse me from these hidden faults...don't let them control me!" Will you humble yourself and do the same? Don't deceive yourself or think more highly of yourself than you ought.

If the enemy can flatter your giftedness and cause you to take your eyes off him, you'll stay bound.

You'll move forward saying things like, "I can't help that I'm able to see things and people as they really are." The truth is, you may be hoodwinked. It takes a mature child of God to deal with the hidden faults no one else can see and because of the integrity of your heart, you refuse to tolerate them.

✳ Slander

Acts 13:45 NLT

But when some of the Jews saw the crowds, they were jealous; so they slandered Paul and argued against whatever he said.

Be careful what you entertain—some come "SHARING" what someone else has done to hurt them, to betray them, to offend them, to wrong them, etc.

But GUARD your heart, what looks or sounds like "SHARING" might actually be "SLANDER!"

Don't participate!!! Don't let the filters of your mind and heart be muddied with someone else's affairs, which you really don't know anything about, except what "they" tell you. I know...we love our brothers and sisters in Christ, we love our family and friends and we want to be there for them and show them our support. However, what may seem like "showing support" can turn into "sowing seeds" of discord.

Your participation begins to promulgate and perpetuate division and the destruction of any possible relationship you could have had with the "alleged perpetrator," thereby cancelling any blessing that would have come along with it. Let us not be deceived by the craftiness of the enemy. Don't let him cause trouble over someone you care about and another person. God may have wanted it to be a divine connection for you, but the enemy was able to destroy the connection before its conception, because he had them meet your "Gehazi" first (2 Kings 5). Don't miss it—read that again! We need Elishas in this season who can discern the truth behind what is being said and what is really being done.

Be careful you are not the one who comes "sharing" when you know your heart isn't in the right place. Don't poison the perception of your friends and loved ones.

✳ Defensive

When we harbor jealousy in our minds and hearts, we can become quite guarded. We put up walls and defenses to "protect" ourselves from the imagined onslaughts of those of whom we are jealous. Everything they say or do is picked apart and the perverted defense system put in place will magnify certain words or actions and turn them into weapons of attack set against you. Now you feel as though you have to attack back leaving the person you are jealous of bewildered and bemused because everything was twisted and taken out of context.

Be careful that your unnecessary defense doesn't make you prey to a spirit of offense.

Keep in mind, jealousy can cause you to overreact. Even though we can give a reason or state a fact, remember when the root of your reaction is jealousy, it is never justified.

✳ Derision

One thing I find disconcerting is the ridicule most men and women of God face as they do His work. The open dislike, disdain and disrespect is daunting.

Many will try to find something wrong with them, with what they say, what they do, questioning their motives, trying to find hidden agendas, criticizing, judging, mocking and accusations. There is fault finding, despising and attempts to totally discredit them.

I beseech you, do not sit in the seat of the scornful. It is a dangerous seat. Be mindful that you are seated in heavenly places with Jesus.

Proverbs 3:34 NKJV
Surely He scorns the scornful,
But gives grace to the humble.

Psalm 1:1 NKJV
Blessed is the man
Who walks not in the counsel of the ungodly,
Nor stands in the path of sinners,
Nor sits in the seat of the scornful;

Let me say it again, get out of that seat—it is a very hot seat.

✳ **Easily Offended**

It is absolutely startling how when a spirit of jealousy (or any spirit for that matter), is in a position of influence and taking advantage of the believer, it has the power to completely change our response, position, behavior, attitude, and even how we see or perceive things. It's amazing how things are actually flipped upside-down, turned inside-out and the appearance of a thing becomes a grave misrepresentation because the lenses we now see through have been muddied and defiled.

(Off)ense can turn you "off" when you would have otherwise been turned on. It will shut down the very things that should have gone forward without any hindrance. Offense will cause you to stand in a place of opposition when you really should be in a place of support. Offense will cause you to tear down when you really should be building up.

Offense will cause you to feel justified in evil-doing. You'll know what the will of the Lord is, but you won't do it because you're offended.

Instead of love and peace guarding your heart, offense will rise up and create a guard for your hurt, your pain, and your bitterness.

✳ Infatuation & Obsessive thoughts

Have you ever noticed how much mental space a person of whom you're jealous begins to occupy? Your thoughts of them increase to an uncomfortable level and you know things have gotten out of hand, but you feel like you're in a trap—in a bad movie that only plays created scenarios of imagined arguments.

It literally feels like you've become infatuated and your thoughts have become obsessive—sometimes you entertain them and go along with yet another instant replay that becomes a saga and sometimes you are frustrated by them. You successfully ignore them for a moment, until the next pop-up movie begins to play.

A lot of arguments take place in your imagination. A LOT! Cast them down. Interrupt them and exalt God's truth! Make up "your mind" that it can't be played with and that you will no longer lend it to a vain imagination. You are not a puppet—cut the strings!

2 Corinthians 10:4-5 NKJV

[4] For the weapons of our warfare are not carnal but mighty in God for pulling down strongholds, [5] casting down arguments and every high thing that exalts itself against the knowledge of God, bringing every thought into captivity to the obedience of Christ,

✴ Insults

When you are jealous, oftentimes, you find yourself insulting the person and the people connected to them. If someone celebrates them or cheers them on in any way—watch out! —a barrage of insults will be hurled at those who support them (pathetic, groupie, desperate, etc.).

This is mostly done in your imagination. God forbid anyone knew what you were thinking.

Be careful what you allow your imagination to entertain. Even your imagination should be set apart for God's use and glory. Don't let it be contaminated with wickedness.

✴ Control

Oftentimes, when you are operating in a spirit of jealousy, you want to be in control. Not only do you want to be the hero, the healer and the anointed one, but if you're not in control, you want to make sure no one else is. You find yourself always wanting to regulate, govern, dictate, lead, or delegate. If someone else is leading, you feel uncomfortable and you either want to leave or shut it all down.

When jealousy and control work together, it's usually your way or the highway. This is often accompanied by a need for power and influence, not knowing that in this state, you are not ready for either one of them and are apt to do more harm than good.

A controlling spirit finds it difficult to collaborate and work together as a team. When a spirit of control is confronted or challenged, it gives way to anger and oftentimes, leaves a person feeling ill-will towards others. You don't want them to prosper, you don't want them to be successful, and inwardly, although you are aware that how you feel isn't right, you sometimes hope the person, ministry, the business or the assignment fails.

When jealousy and control work together, you oftentimes find yourself wanting the credit, recognition, praise and accolades. You want the titles, the positions and the respect that comes along with them.

Control wants to have power over people and things and wants to rule, but be careful because God says it is better to be patient than powerful, better to have "self-control" than to conquer a city (Proverbs 16:32 NLT).

Don't partner with this spirit. Let go and let God have His way. Let God appoint whom He wills and humble yourself before Him. There's a time to lead and there's a time to be led. Don't fight against those He has chosen. Do your part and let others do theirs. It's time to restore the unity.

✳ The Disqualifier

In the body of Christ at large, we must grow out of that diseased mentality which seeks to disqualify everyone God is using. No matter how anointed they are and how clearly God is using them, something in us wants to find something in them to discount what they do and discredit what they say.

In this hour, we really need to learn how to do Colossians 3:12-15. We really need to start showing more grace, knowing we are all growing and running our race with God's help. We don't need our own brothers and sisters in the faith pointing out flaws, weaknesses, and places where we've fallen short. If God can cheer us on, say get up and keep going, why are we ok with trying to shut each other down?

I can't imagine what this generation would do with Apollos whom God sent, who was teaching greatly, but didn't know anything about the Holy Spirit. We really need to take heed to how Aquila and Priscilla handled the situation. They gently informed him about what he was missing, full of love and grace, instead of trying to disqualify him, calling him a false teacher and shutting down his ministry.

Acts 18:25-26 NLT
[25] He had been taught the way of the Lord, and he taught others about Jesus with an enthusiastic spirit and with accuracy. However, he knew only about John's baptism. [26] When Priscilla and Aquila heard him preaching boldly in the synagogue, they took him aside and explained the way of God even more accurately.

We have to understand, not just when it comes to our walk with the Lord, but also for our brothers and sisters, that God gives us the truth in pieces, He doesn't give it to us all at once. So, let's be more gracious and support one another in love, because no matter how great we are as individuals, we NEED each other.

✳ Attention! Attention!

Attention! No, really...attention! Have you ever noticed that when someone else is getting attention, your need or desire for attention begins to stir? All of a sudden, as the other person is receiving the attention, your patience starts to wear thin, you become irritated, aggravated and frustrated?

If the attention shifts to you, or it becomes your turn to speak and be heard, your turn to perform and be seen, all of a sudden you feel a thousand times better and all the pressure that was building and threatening to boil over is no longer present.

On the flip side, what if your turn never comes in that situation, that hour, that day or even that season? How will you handle it? You can sit there and grow in frustration, feel all messed up inside, jealous and just plain bothered, and allow those thoughts and emotions to grow. If you know like I know, it gets way out of hand and next thing you know your imagination becomes vain and false scenarios are being created, further stirring your emotions. Your imagination creates plays, plots, additional players and climaxes that end in someone's destruction.

We must stop being attention seekers and wanting the spotlight to shine on us. We have to come to a place, where we not only recognize that God is doing great things through all of us, but also accept, step back and be willing to applaud someone else.

IRRATIONAL THINKING | IRRATIONAL SPEAKING

Oftentimes, in the process of looking at someone else's life, we begin to think irrationally and speak irrationally. It usually comes in the form of a question or questions. Our thoughts are bombarded with a boat load of questions including "whys" and "how comes." You know how we do when we're completely fed up: Why is my life stuck in the balances? Where is my mentor? Why don't I have anyone who is able to help me? Why don't I have anyone who can impart into my life? Where is my wise counsel? Where is my Godly counsel? Where are the apostles who are going to watch over my life? Where are the prophets in my life? How come my life feels like it's not going anywhere? How come I feel stuck? Why is it that I feel like nothing I do works? Why does it feel like everything falls through for me? Why does it feel like my life is so unfruitful? Why does it feel like I'm on the sidelines watching everybody else? God why aren't you coming through for me? Where is my help? Where is my breakthrough? When is it going to be my time?

One thing I noticed that I think is a little backwards is that when we see or hear about someone doing well, we get jealous—we get upset, envious or bitter. On the other hand, when we see or hear about somebody doing badly or suffering misfortune, we all of a sudden become grateful— "Oh God, I'm glad that You are watching over me; I'm glad You love me; I'm glad You are protecting me and my family. God I'm glad Your hand is upon me; I'm glad Your hedge of protection is round about me..." We get really grateful and thankful. Why does it take someone's misfortunes for us to be grateful and count our blessings?

Could it be that it should be the other way around? When we see somebody doing good and we see them doing well, we can still be grateful and thankful and praise our God for how good He is to us in the midst of being good for someone else. Amen!

Let us make this a common practice. It may take some time and many do-overs until we get it right—but we will get it right. We won't stop until we get it right. The next time we hear or see someone doing well and God blessing them, instead of getting jealous, we're going to count our blessings and thank Him. Grab yourself an accountability partner and get comfortable in this change.

DON'T LET JEALOUSY BLOCK YOUR BLESSINGS

Be careful you don't allow jealousy to cause you not to receive from one of your brothers or sisters in Christ. We know that God uses His children. We know that the Word says to each one is given the manifestation of the Spirit to profit withal. We know that there are mighty men and women of God. We know that there are many who are doing the work. We know that there are many who are anointed, many God is using, many who are going

forth, many who are working miracles, signs and won-
ders, many who preach well, and teach well. There are
many who prophesy, many who operate in the gifts of the
Spirit and many who are led by the Spirit. The way God is
using them is extremely beneficial to the body of Christ.

However, oftentimes, when we become jealous of a person, we decide that we don't want what they have to offer.
I want you to be careful because if you are in a position
where you can receive from this person, but you choose
not to because of jealousy, you may miss the very thing
God wants to release to you in that moment. It could be
divinely orchestrated to bless your life; whether it's a
word, a miracle, a prophecy, a word of wisdom, instruction, or direction. If you decide that you don't want to listen, you don't want to hear, you don't want to read about
it, you don't want to go, and you don't want to know,
because you are jealous, you could be circumventing a
gift from God.

I want us to be in a place where we can receive whatever God is doing and whoever He is using. If you recognize God is truly using that person, I want you to be
able to position yourself to receive in the name of Jesus.
Now, if you don't know whether or not God is using that
person, but they're getting praise, influence, open doors,
people are cheering them on and you're sitting there jealous, you do not have to receive. However, you do want to
be sure. It will behoove you to ask, "God are you using

this person?" Tell Him, "God, I don't want to miss what You are doing!" Repent and ask Him to forgive you. Again, God uses His children! You don't want to be in a position where you are not able to receive.

✳ The Critic

Besides our unwillingness to receive from the anointing on someone's life, we'll oftentimes take on a critical spirit that will seemingly justify why we can't receive from them. We'll inwardly criticize the way they speak, from their accent and dialect to the misuse and mispronunciation of words. We'll criticize the way they dress, the way they look, the way they walk or carry themselves. We'll take the minute and shed light on it—any negative thing we can find, we'll highlight it to abase them.

This in turn causes us to dishonor, disrespect and discount certain people because of our inward struggle with a spirit of jealousy. Be careful who you decide to dishonor. Be careful who you decide to disrespect. There can be consequences of which you are not aware besides the obvious missing out on a blessing. Give honor where honor is due and check that spirit of jealousy. Don't let it have dominion over you and cause you to wreak havoc in your own life.

I don't know if you've ever experienced when a spirit has just gone too far and overplayed its hand, so much so that it forces you to deal with it. I have with a spirit of heaviness and I was forced to confront it. We are at a critical point in the body of Christ at large where this spirit of jealousy is just doing too much and the people of God must arise, take authority and subdue it.

3

GUARD YOUR RELATIONSHIPS

Declaration: I will walk in love and be intentional about not allowing jealousy to destroy my relationships! I'm on Guard!

GUARD THE GIFT

It is imperative for us to begin to guard our relationships. They are gifts to us from a loving Father. We have tremendously undervalued each other and have been in the mindset of, "I can take her or leave her," "she can come or she can go." Because we have not properly valued one another, the enemy has been able to come in and steal this precious gift.

The enemy knows that one can put a thousand to flight and two can put ten thousand to flight. Why would he want us to stand together? He also knows that many are lovers of themselves, selfish, unfaithful and uncommitted. So, all he needs to do is stir up a little bit of trouble and we will cut each other off—we will quickly end the relationship. Is your sister in Christ not worth fighting for? Is she really that unvaluable to you? In these last days, we need to go in with the mindset that we're going to fight for our relationships. We will not be easily irritated or easily offended. We will not be unforgiving.

There is much to gain in loving each other and walking in agreement. Your sisters have value—they have worth.

LET'S TAKE THIS HEAD ON!

It is unfortunate that the very thing we crave as humans is the very thing we participate in destroying in the body of Christ—RELATIONSHIPS. We earnestly desire—at the core of our being—good, genuine relationships that are filled with love, peace, joy and encouragement. Godly relationships become places where we are safe, strengthened, loved unconditionally, free to be the unique masterpiece God created us to be and are in turn celebrated and encouraged to succeed. We receive support and Godly counsel in Godly relationships.

Why then are we so okay with our relationships being torn down and ripped apart?

Why are we okay with division when we know God wants us to dwell together in unity?

What's more disheartening is that we come up with fads and sayings that further support the separation and severing of Godly relationships, when in fact, we are one body jointly fit together. The eye is not supposed to say to the foot, "I don't need you!" Yet, we come up with sayings like, "God is separating us because everybody can't go where I am going!" Well, let me ask you this: Where are you going? Where are you going as a hand that your foot can't come along? This is serious!

When did God ever need to use strife, contention, petty arguments and quarreling to separate to Himself a person to do good works?

Everything will be going well in a relationship, then jealousy enters—envy, offense, hurt, misunderstandings—and all of a sudden, you want to end the relationship. If this is the case, please stop putting God's name on it, saying He's promoting you or taking you higher.

Let's look at what a God-ordained separation looks like using the experience of Paul and Barnabas.

Acts 13:2-4a NLT

2 One day as these men were worshiping the Lord and fasting, the Holy Spirit said, "Appoint Barnabas and Saul for the special work to which I have called them." 3 So after more fasting and prayer, the men laid their hands on them and sent them on their way. 4 So Barnabas and Saul were sent out by the Holy Spirit.

Can you see how this is a God-ordained separation for a season? There weren't any relationships severed. There wasn't any strife, animosity, jealousy, offense or contention. With the separation came blessings and God's grace. Paul and Barnabas were sent out by the Holy Spirit. Everybody in their circle knew it and were in agreement.

As a matter of fact, when the special work that Paul and Barnabas were sent to do was completed, we find that they returned to the same group of believers eager to share testimonies and reports about everything God accomplished through them. Hallelujah! Isn't it wonderful to be able to come back home and have people with whom you can share your experiences? Isn't it a blessing to have a group of supporters who are excited about how God is using you and are just as eager to celebrate the goodness of the Lord with you? Furthermore, how critical is it to have believers, your brothers and sisters in Christ, covering you in prayer as you complete the work God sent you to do?

Let's look at what happened when they returned.

Acts 14:26-28 (NLT)

[26] Finally, they returned by ship to Antioch of Syria, where their journey had begun. The believers there had entrusted them to the grace of God to do the work they had now completed. [27] Upon arriving in Antioch, they called the church together and reported everything God had done through them and how he had opened the door of faith to the Gentiles, too. [28] And they stayed there with the believers for a long time.

Can I get an Amen! We need to renew our minds and start walking in the true love of Christ that is patient and long-suffering, full of mercy and grace.

When we look at the relationship Jesus had with His disciples, He wasn't getting rid of them and replacing them with other people. He never told Peter he was doing too much and that he couldn't be a part of His team anymore. He never told "doubting" Thomas that He didn't like his attitude and have to cut all ties with him.

If anybody could say they were going higher in God and certain people couldn't go with them, it would be Jesus. However, Jesus said no such thing! On the contrary, He prayed to the Father and told Him He wanted His disciples to be with Him where He was. He told them that where He was going, He was preparing a place for them too. Thank You Lord! Why then are we comfortable saying it's the heart and plan of God to go cutting people off when God isn't in that plan? The heart of God has always been for a united Church—for us to be as one.

John 17:20-24 (NLT)

[20] "I am praying not only for these disciples but also for all who will ever believe in me through their message. [21] I pray that they will all be one, just as you and I are one— as you are in me, Father, and I am in you. And may they be in us so that the world will believe you sent me.

[22] "I have given them the glory you gave me, so they may be one as we are one. [23] I am in them and you are in me. May they experience such perfect unity that the world will know that you sent me and that you love them as much as you love me. [24] Father, I want these whom you have given me to be with me where I am. Then they can see all the glory you gave me because you loved me even before the world began!

Can you see and feel the heart of God?

GREATER LEVEL OF MATURITY

We need to walk in a greater level of maturity. What does this look like?

✓ We need to be completely filled with the love of God and let it do what the Word of God said it could do: cover a multitude of sins.

✓ We need to be quick to forgive—please stop holding on to stuff. What right do you have to condemn someone whom God has forgiven?

✓ We need to stop demanding our own way—stop falling out and throwing tantrums when somebody doesn't agree with you or want to do things your way. It's time to put away childish things and childish behavior. You can't continue to stomp your feet and fold your arms— stubbornly creating tension and division.

✓ We need to stop thinking more highly of ourselves than we ought. Humble ourselves and consider others as greater. If this makes you feel small and insignificant, you may need inner healing.

✓ We need to show mercy and compassion.

✓ We need to be slow to anger. Check your attitude— if you are still at a place in your emotions where anger is quickly aroused and you are easily frustrated, easily irritated and easily aggravated, you may not be rooted in love. Make this your prayer before God—that you would be more deeply rooted in the love of Christ, that you would be filled with the love that comes with Christ

Jesus and that His love would be shed abroad in your heart.

Proverbs 19:11 ESV

Good sense makes one slow to anger,
   and it is his glory to overlook an offense.

Proverbs 14:29 NLT

People with understanding control their anger;
   a hot temper shows great foolishness.

✓ We need to be slow to speak and quick to listen. This is worth repeating...SLOOOOW TO SPEAK and QUICK TO LISTEN!

✓ We need to be peace-makers.

Matthew 5:9 KJV

Blessed are the peacemakers: for they shall be called the children of God.

God has given us the commandment to love each other.

John 13:34 NLT

So now I am giving you a new commandment: Love each other. Just as I have loved you, you should love each other.

Can we get back to love?

There is a popular question now in the body of Christ: Have you learned to love?

The truth is—many haven't. Many are broken and wounded and come from various backgrounds of dysfunction. We have so many roots that aren't rooted in Christ. It is from these hurting places that we learn to have relationships, however false or dysfunctional.

Have you learned to love?
Have you learned to love?
Have you learned to love?

THE AFTERMATH OF RELATIONSHIPS DESTROYED

Most of us have experienced feelings or run-ins with jealousy. Sometimes these feelings are aroused by people we have never actually met, other times, by acquaintances and oftentimes, they are aroused by those we love and care for. The latter are the people with whom we really hoped to have had a great relationship or friendship. It is this kind of jealousy that causes the most damage—jealousy between those we know, trust and value.

Jealousy destroys relationships! We have already seen from the very Word of God that jealousy is dangerous. What does it look like when destruction is birthed? What kind of effect does it have? Let's peek in on one possible scenario from the back-end and see why it is imperative that we are diligent to guard our gift of relationship. We'll call this "Linda's Experience:"

In Linda's attempt to get away from June, the one who invoked, provoked, stirred up and aroused a spirit of jealousy, she wanted to disconnect from every other person, group, event or thing to which June was connected.

She went through the thought process where disconnecting was merely a consideration. She thought about how it would make her look if she did and weighed the pros and cons. She came to the conclusion it was best for her to just leave because she couldn't handle or didn't know how to deal with the emotional turmoil the spirit of jealousy had stirred up. Her very own thoughts about June had become a distraction, even to her relationship with God because of the mental torment. It quickly progressed and became a source of frustration. The negative began to outweigh the positive. Any benefit the relationship provided was now tainted, smeared and no longer held the same value to Linda. So finally, she decided to let it go.

Does any part of this sounds familiar, makes sense or sheds light?

Once a relationship is destroyed and there is no more life flowing from it, everything connected to that relationship struggles to survive and death is eminent.

Consequently, you may be left to deal with those taunting thoughts that you were wrong (which may or may not be true) for cutting off the relationship. These thoughts tell you that you're on the short end of the stick now, you're going to miss out, you're going to regret it, or those other connections could have really been a benefit to you, etc. You may wonder if you were foolish or if you look foolish. You may wonder what others are saying about you and if they're making you look bad amongst others? Then what may follow are the mocking thoughts that they're not thinking about you at all, you leaving was of no consequence and the only one affected by your departure was you. Ouch! If you had not already at this point cut off the other connections, you may be tempted to see for yourself whether or not they simply moved on with life and if they are not only doing well but doing better.

Then you may go through another cycle of wondering, after it is all said and done, where you now stand in the grand scheme of life and your journey with God. Yes—it is that serious to you—because likely, you have not yet been perfected in God's love, you have not yet had your soul restored or your mind renewed. The wounds of your heart and soul have not yet been healed and you probably still struggle with how you see yourself.

The spirit of jealousy hates to see the one you're in or were in relationship with, thriving in relationship with others. The spirit of jealousy is a territorial spirit that's easily threatened. It causes insecurities that may have been well hidden to come to the surface. Insecurities make demands to be accommodated. When they are accommodated, relationships become even more dysfunctional and the state of those relationships become increasingly worse until eventually they self-destruct.

Wow! Let's take a breath on this note.

AHHH...SO YOU ENDED UP CUTTING THEM OFF

Jealousy got the best of you for the moment and you behaved in ways that you might regret, you said things you know you shouldn't have, you burned bridges you wish you hadn't, etc. Let's face it—you realize that the one who ended up getting hurt from that silent destroyer was you. It's ok. Let me say it again...IT'S OK! We all make mistakes. Own it, repent, if you did something that needs to be forgiven, apologize and move on.

Let me tell you this: Before you make moves to make amends and right wrongs, go to God in prayer. In prayer, cover the situation and all parties involved. If you decide this process involves other people GET RID OF ALL EXPECTATIONS YOU MAY HAVE! You can hope for the best, but not everyone is going to respond well, not everyone may be willing to forgive, not everyone would be willing to pick up where you left off. Some ties may be cut.

You've decided to sever relationships, now it's time to fill those empty spaces. Wash them with the blood of Jesus and fill them with the goodness of the Lord.

Don't leave them open for the enemy to fill or to be filled with works of the flesh.

Do not be dismayed. There are consequences to our actions and there may be a price to pay for anything you may have said or done. Respect those who decide they would rather move on without you. Yes, it may hurt and you may feel rejected, but stay prayerful, hopeful and keep your head up as you walk out of the grips of jealousy. It's a lesson learned and there will be other chances for creating, building and maintaining healthy relationships.

Remember, God is a restorer! Do your part, whatever is required of you and move on without guilt or condemnation. Leave it in God's hands.

TO TELL OR NOT TO TELL

Should I let my friend or loved one know that I have jealousy toward them? Not really. Not everyone is rooted in Christ enough to handle that truth, so it could possibly cause more harm than good should you choose to divulge this information. Some of your healing and deliverance is between you and God. Even the most mature in the Spirit may struggle after coming into the knowledge that there is jealousy in your heart and you don't want to create unnecessary warfare for them—having to now filter everything you say and do through this knowledge.

Some people may have a difficult time keeping this to themselves, feeling like they are a hypocrite or behaving deceptively. Let me ask you this...up until this point, have you been hypocritical and deceiving? You know where you are and it's time to be completely honest with yourself. If you need to ask your friend or loved one to excuse you for a period of time while you seek the Lord for healing, by all means do so. In this way, you can preserve the relationship. When you come back healed, delivered, set free and restored, the relationship can take on a new level of health and vitality and begin to thrive in a new way.

FROM WHERE DOES YOUR SIGNIFICANCE COME?

Significance = A "Sign if i can ce (see)" myself as God sees me.

The ability to see ourselves as God sees us is critical as we journey through life with God and with others.

Our significance doesn't come from who we are connected to or the amount of things we have or don't have. The problem is when we extract and syphon our significance from people and things. We feel good about ourselves so as long as things are going well. The moment something is said or done that threatens our sense of significance instead of feeding it, we're ready to walk away and the value we've gained from the relationships or the possessions threatens to go away with them.

When you've placed this level of false responsibility on people and the relationship comes to an end because of jealousy, you're left trying to redefine who you are and re-estimate your sense of value and self-worth. Consequently, you may also feel the need to take back everything you've contributed to those relationships. You take back your support—whether it's emotional, social, or financial, etc. You decide you are no longer going to support the ministry, you're no longer going to support the business, the project, the assignment, or the work.

RELATIONSHIPS ARE A GIFT

I'm going to highlight various relationship types in which jealousy tends to breed in order to continue laying a foundation from which to springboard.

I want you to keep in mind that although my focus is not on romantic jealousies, I urge you not to tolerate any form of it. So if you struggle in this area or any other area not mentioned, recognize it and come out of agreement with it.

This book couldn't possibly contain every possible scenario, situation or circumstance; however, my hope is to bring a keen awareness, charge you to be sober and vigilant against this spirit. My hope is to bring unity to the body of Christ and glory to God.

Here are some of the relationships that jealousy tends to affect:

o Siblings
o Friends
o Co-laborers in ministry
o Co-workers in the marketplace
o New converts or newly planted
o Leaders of other leaders

o Strangers
o Leaders of their sheep
o Sheep of their leaders
o Sheep of other sheep

o Enemies

o Neighbors

✳ Siblings

Often referred to as sibling rivalry, these relationships are usually our first experiences. They are also the places where we've messed up the most and taken one another for granted. This is not just rampant amongst blood relatives, but brothers and sisters in the body of Christ.

Jealousy creates rivalry. We've fought against one another long enough. Your portion is supposed to be a family of those whom you love and support and who love and support you.

✶ Friends

How heartbreaking is it to have a relationship, which once thrived in love, great times, acceptance, companionship, time spent, memorable experiences created, secrets shared, and tears shed on shoulders, abruptly end because jealousy came in and was never effectively dealt with?

There are too many of us who hold the testimony that finding a friend is difficult, while on the same hand, really desiring to have one.

Friends are important and so very special. They make a huge difference in our lives and are immeasurably valuable. I'm grateful for the many who have this blessing.

Proverbs 18:24 NLT & NKJV

24 There are "friends" **who** destroy each other,
but a real friend sticks closer than a brother.

24 A man who has friends must himself be friendly,
But there is a friend **who** sticks closer than a brother.

Let's really begin to show ourselves friendly. Don't be afraid to open your heart. Don't be afraid to be vulnerable. Pray—ask God for wisdom, discernment and LOVE.

✳ Co-laborers in ministry

Oh, how great it is for brethren to dwell together in unity! It is so rewarding to find your place in the body of Christ, to begin serving and working for the Lord, going deeper in the things of God, bringing Him glory, operating in the gifts of the Holy Spirit, demonstrating the power of God, doing great exploits, and being fruitful in good works. This is what we pray for—for ourselves and for others in our private time with God. We pray for God to raise up those who will do these things and more. So, why is it that when we see our prayers answered and our brothers and sisters flourishing and prospering, we allow a spirit of jealousy to infiltrate our camps? Why have we allowed this spirit to come in and take a seat as if it belongs?

It is a tremendous blessing to co-labor amongst one another.

Matthew 12:48-50 NLT
[48] Jesus asked, "Who is my mother? Who are my brothers?" [49] Then he pointed to his disciples and said, "Look, these are my mother and brothers. [50] Anyone who does

the will of my Father in heaven is my brother and sister and mother!"

✳ Co-workers in the marketplace

We are used to the competitive nature of the marketplace. When we applied for the job, there were countless others who also applied. When we were invited to interview for the job, there were others who received the same invitation even though there was only one position to be filled. We looked at our best, we spoke our best, we did our best and we conducted ourselves in a professional manner. All in hopes of the job being offered to us.

Once we're on the job, sometimes it's just you as the one-woman show and other times, there are many performing the same job and there are reports and metrics to monitor and assess how you perform in relation to how others are performing.

Somehow, it seems like a direct insult to us when a co-worker receives recognition for being a top performer, for achieving optimal results, for hitting targets and reaching or exceeding goals, or for being promoted and climbing the corporate ladder.

Jealousy will cause you to hate that your co-worker is receiving such positive attention and affirmation. It bothers you to see them succeeding and somehow, you would begin to turn inward and wonder why you weren't good enough for the promotion. This spirit robs you of your desire and ability to celebrate the blessing someone else is receiving.

Be careful of anything that would cause you to compare and conclude that you don't measure up.

Be careful that a sense of entitlement doesn't rise, with subsequent feelings of bitterness, convincing you that you haven't been awarded equal opportunity to be where they are or to have what they have acquired. These feelings insinuate that you've been intentionally overlooked and people are against you. You begin to have such thoughts as, "If I had what she had given to 'me' I would be 'that' too;" "If I was going around brown-nosing as much as she did, I'm sure I would've received a promotion too," etc.

Don't let the lies of jealousy create things that become "truth" only to you; ultimately, feeling like you have to set yourself apart as a lone ranger.

Be mindful that this can happen in any area of your life or any group of which you're a part.

✳ Neighbors

Yes, here are prime examples of how we magically see our neighbors' grass as greener than our own. Somehow their marriage looks like they could have their own television show. Their children seem to be doing exceptionally well. They have the best jobs, the best cars, and influential social circles. They take the best vacations and your life just seems to dull in comparison.

This simple prepositional phrase, "in comparison," seems to create a road that leads down a path straight into a world of inner turmoil and outer destruction. Avoid this road at all costs and come out of that place of comparison.

✳ Enemies

Most people don't want to see their enemies prosper.

Psalm 37:1 NKJV
Do not fret because of evildoers,
Nor be envious of the workers of iniquity.

Don't fret, stop getting worked up when you see people prospering and they're not saved. Stop thinking about how unfair it is, for God knows all things.

Matthew 5:45 NLT

In that way, you will be acting as true children of your Father in heaven. For He gives His sunlight to both the evil and the good, and He sends rain on the just and the unjust alike.

Proverbs 16:7 NKJV
When a man's ways please the LORD,
He makes even his enemies to be at peace with him.

As I mentioned earlier, jealousy will turn people into enemies. Be careful that you don't allow it to turn you into a secret enemy—cheerleading outwardly and jealous and hating inwardly.

Let me emphatically state this—your brothers and sisters in Christ are not your enemies. They may be used by the enemy, but remember who your real enemy is.

Ephesians 6:12 NKJV
For we do not wrestle against flesh and blood, but against principalities, against powers, against the rulers of the darkness of this age, against spiritual hosts of wickedness in the heavenly places.

PRAY! PRAY! PRAY!

We have been made a family through Jesus Christ, don't be okay with your brothers and sisters bound by jealousy and oppressed by the enemy.

Do your part to keep the peace and unity.

✳ Strangers

We have unfortunately experienced jealousy by people we have never met. Strangers include: celebrities and public figures (secular and non-secular). Those we know of by social media who have the appearance of success, happiness, riches, material possessions, love, peace, purpose, confidence, and favor with God and with man. The list goes on.

✳ Leaders of their Sheep

Let's face it, the sons and daughters of the Most High God, our God, are called to do great works and bring Him glory. They have the same Holy Spirit you have, they have access to God and the secret place of God, just as you do. They are empowered to be filled with the fruit of the Spirit and are encouraged to operate in the gifts of the Spirit, just as you are. Take heed of your attitude, actions, responses and your heart concerning your sheep. If when they are being used by God, insecurity is being stirred up in you and you feel the need to control them by stunting them and shutting them down, then jealousy may be in operation.

If you feel like using your authority as their leader to stop their flow or if you feel undoubtedly intimidated by the grace on their lives, which you haven't yet seen in your own, make sure you take the time to bring this matter before God in prayer.

If you feel threatened and find yourself trying to trump everything they say, trump everything they do and find yourself feeling compelled to let everyone know you're the one in charge, there is a serious issue. Your role as a leader is not to compete, but to lead, govern, oversee, support, encourage, build up and even serve, doing it all with and in the love of Christ.

✳ Sheep of their Leaders

Have you ever "felt some kind of way" when your leader or leadership was teaching, preaching, counseling, or encouraging and you began to have such thoughts as, "I could have said that better," "I thought he/she was going to go in another direction with that message?" Somehow, afterwards, you're now a little disappointed or further convinced that you simply could have said it better or done a better job. Be careful because you may be operating in jealousy.

Have you ever wondered why you felt the urge to compare?

Be careful! If this isn't checked and dealt with, it could lead to a complete loss of honor and respect for your leaders or those in leadership.

Furthermore, it could land you in a position where you become unteachable and you are no longer open to receive from them.

This could be a dangerous place to be in if God planted you in that house to grow, to be strengthened, and to serve, but your heart is in a place where you are no longer submitted or subservient.

Pay attention to your attitude and your behavior towards them and see if you always find yourself critiquing what they say and do or how they say and do it.

Pay attention to whether you become fault finding and "easily" able to detect their errors (which may not be of the Lord); if you show little to no mercy; you always question their decisions; or you are always in a place where you "just don't agree."

Don't tolerate these things, but be quick to bring them before God in prayer, be willing to adjust your attitude and do not harden your heart.

✳ Leaders of other Leaders

It is unfortunate that many leaders feel alone and isolated as if they don't have anyone to support them as they do the work of the Lord. They can't share their burdens with their sheep, they feel as though others in leadership wouldn't understand what they are going through or that they would be harshly judged. Many leaders simply do not feel safe with other leaders.

There is so much competition and comparing the size of churches and ministries—comparing the level of impact in a city, comparing levels of influence, and power. It has almost literally become a popularity contest. Now that social media is in the mix, the competition for a great following (for the wrong reasons) is out of hand.

There is jealousy over connections, membership, buildings, land, and success in business and in ministry.

Today we find many leaders pointing out the flaws and weaknesses of others. Please take a good look at what is written concerning how Aquila and Priscilla handled Apollos and govern yourselves accordingly.

2 Corinthians 6:3-4 NLT
[3] We live in such a way that no one will stumble because of us, and no one will find fault with our ministry.
[4] In everything we do, we show that we are true ministers of God. We patiently endure troubles and hardships and calamities of every kind.

You were created to withstand and overcome the pressures and not to succumb to them. If you are already weary, weakened and wrought by various kinds of pressures, that in itself can make you susceptible to this spirit of jealousy. These pressures—pressure to perform, be perfect, meet the demands of the people, meet your own expectations, etc. can be very destructive. An inability to properly handle pressure can push you in the wrong direction, press you to compare and compete, pull you into all kinds of ungodly behavior and cause you to pour out of your soul instead of the Spirit of God.

Please set yourself to unite and support other leaders. Do not be one who sows discord in the family of God. You have been entrusted with a great responsibility. Many have been entrusted to govern the sheep, so we must be sure that we govern ourselves accordingly. It is hard work to say the least and your brothers and sisters could use your support and encouragement.

✳ Sheep of other Sheep

Oftentimes, jealousy manifests when you see your leader, pastor, apostle, or teacher, pouring into another member of the group, church, ministry, etc. You witness another member or person receiving encouragement, being told how loved they are, all that God has for them, all that God is doing in their lives and how He favors them.

You see the leader training them, giving them extra personal time, helping them, exhorting them, strengthening them and all of a sudden, you start feeling some kind of way (jealous) and the famous question is posed: "WHAT ABOUT ME!!!!?"

And then it starts: comparisons...dreadful! You start comparing how the leader treats you compared to how they treat the other person. You start comparing what they did or didn't do for you versus them. You start comparing the amount of time they give you versus them.

And more often than not, you come out with the short end of the stick, right?

And now...you have a valid case against the leader... after all, it's not just you "feeling" this way, you compared and you have proof.

Have you considered the fact that the other person may actually need that extra attention or encouragement? I know...before you say, "But I do too!" - let me share with you something that has helped me:

1 Kings 3:8-9 NKJV

[8] And Your servant is in the midst of Your people whom You have chosen, a great people, too numerous to be numbered or counted. [9] Therefore give to Your servant an understanding heart to judge Your people, that I may

discern between good and evil. For who is able to judge this great people of Yours?"

We have to keep in mind exactly what Solomon said to God, "Your servant is in the midst of "YOUR PEOPLE..." We are always grateful to the shepherds God has given us after His own heart and we should always respect and honor them. However, I want to encourage you not to forget that we belong to God—we are "His" responsibility. He has promised to take care of us and provide for us and to lead us into all truth and teach us in the way that we should go. I say this to say, be cognizant of the expectations you place on your leaders. Sometimes our very own ill-placed expectations create disappointment and open the door to offense.

Don't make it hard for your leaders. As we've seen with Solomon, the people are numerous, the needs of the people can't even be counted. We know how much people pull on our leaders and it can be overwhelming. Pray for them and go to God for yourself in prayer to see how He wants things to be handled. In this way, you'll be of great help to your leaders and not a hindrance (I'm not saying never go to your leaders for you know as much as I do, we NEED prayer and Godly counsel).

Try not to be selfish and make demands of their time and allow them to give proper attention to others in need and ask God how you can be of assistance—you may very well be needed in prayer.

More often than not, the root of jealousy against other sheep in the house has nothing to do with the treatment received from the leaders. Oftentimes, it is simply the person—their call, their anointing, their confidence, their looks, their social status, or their success. It can be downright miserable to serve in the same place as someone of whom you're jealous. All hope is not lost and this too shall pass. I encourage you to quickly and persistently get before God and like Jacob, don't let Him go until He blesses you—until you get your deliverance. Don't let Him go until you come out radiating with the assurance of His love for you.

ADDRESSING AN ELEPHANT

Leaders it's imperative that you don't birth a breeding ground for jealousy by boasting about your personal relationship with one of your sheep to your other sheep. It doesn't need to be flaunted or paraded. This type of behavior will create a mess of a myriad of symptoms for which it will take discernment and the help of God to guide you to the root cause of all the issues breaking out. Very few people will come right out and admit they're jealous. It may look like all manner of acting out, disobedience, unteachableness, strange behavior, undependable, unfaithful, offense, anger, bitterness, etc.

The fact is, oftentimes these feelings are hidden and the sheep are embarrassed by them. Since the jealousy was stirred or caused by your behavior, they won't feel comfortable coming to you for help with the dilemma, so they will try to ignore it. However, now that the door has been opened, much of what is said or done by you and received by them is filtered through the jealousy they don't even want to admit is there. Now, there is this unspoken, unwanted and unnecessary warfare the sheep is undergoing within themselves and they don't know how to effectively go it alone and secure the victory of overcoming jealousy. It's a great day for breakthrough!

2 Corinthians 6:3 NLT
We live in such a way that no one will stumble because of us, and no one will find fault with our ministry.

I will give honorable mention to the "friend" of the leader who is in the middle of this silent battle who may have to endure the strange behavior or ill-treatment from others simply because they hold the coveted position of "friend."

Let us all be careful, be mindful, and be wise in our dealings and in our roles as leaders, as God has entrusted His sheep to you. We do not want to be responsible for sowing seeds of discord.

NEW CONVERTS OR NEWLY PLANTED

For some reason, we have an expectation or an idea that new people are going to be less experienced and/ or less "gifted." We sometimes don't expect them to come in more experienced than we are or stronger. We have become used to having to "train" if you will, those who are new to the team or group and get them acclimated to the environment and caught up to speed with where the group is and where it is going. We half-way don't expect them to come in, hit the ground running, and begin to shift things and teach us.

However, in a healthy body, we have to be mindful that new people aren't necessarily new to the Faith, the work or the gifts of the Spirit. We're used to having to make concessions for those who are less experienced, but we're not necessarily used to or even comfortable with those who come in as our seniors. When this happens, instead of appreciating what they bring to strengthen the whole house, we become threatened and our attitudes show it.

Whether it be a new convert or someone being newly planted into the group, the ministry, the company, etc., we don't want them to feel uncomfortable, unwanted or unwelcome because we feel threatened. This is one of the reasons why many don't want to be associated with the "church." In their experience, "church" people are some of the meanest, most hateful, and most spiteful people they know and the last thing they feel is the love of Christ or acceptance.

In this space, we also have to be careful with how we respond to the promotion of those with whom we are familiar. Let me give you an example. I worked at a bank as an underwriter. As an underwriter, there are people we work with who are in a supportive role, called processors. The underwriter is used to the processor first obtaining information needed from the customer, for the underwriter to effectively complete their job. If any additional information is needed, it is the processor who goes back to the customer to have that conversation.

As with any job or role of responsibility, people want to grow. They learn all they can in the position they're in, they perform well and when an opportunity comes along for them to get promoted into a higher role, they apply. They go through the interview process, are offered the job, leave their "old" position and step into the "new." In the new position, they are no longer responsible for the old things, and someone else will come along to fill that space. They now, fully occupy and are responsible for doing the work of the new position.

Oftentimes, the new position comes with new responsibilities and new benefits. Their title changes and so does their job description. No one expects them to still be available to do the old job. Oftentimes, they are even

celebrated by both their old and new team members—
one saying good-bye and sharing their excitement about
the new opportunity and the other group welcoming them
aboard and offering assistance for them to be successful
in their new position.

What I really want to touch on here is when we as individuals have gotten used to the person being in a certain role or position of "support" and now they have been
promoted to "our" level. How do we treat them? Do we
celebrate with them? Do we offer our assistance so that
they can prosper in their new position? What are our expectations of them and do those expectations line up with
what God is calling them to accomplish? Are we under-
estimating them? Are we threatened by them? When they
come in doing very well, do we become jealous of them?
When they matriculate through their process and it looks
like they're "surpassing" us, and moving into leadership
positions, what is our attitude like?

We have to keep in mind that God knows the plans He
has for each and every one of us. Someone may serve in
the same capacity as you for a season, but it may not be
their final destination. They are going through their process of becoming all that God called them to be just as
you are. It may look like their "come-up" was all of a sudden, but the truth of the matter is, before the foundation
of the world, God knew them and created works for them
to walk in. Don't be thrown off by temporary assignments

designed to bring people into their next and be tempted to put a lid on them because they were once in a subordinate role and now they're in leadership. Don't get in the way of what God is doing. Be prayerful and be wise.

GOD ADDS TO THE VINEYARD

The parable of the vineyard workers in Matthew 20 is another great example of how we sometimes treat each other.

"For the Kingdom of Heaven is like the landowner who went out early one morning to hire workers for his vineyard. ² He agreed to pay the normal daily wage and sent them out to work.

Let me interject here for a moment. How many of us who are chosen by God and sent out to do the work He called us to do, are reaping the blessings, benefits, rewards, and gifts He lavishes upon us, are also getting distracted by the wages other people are receiving?

Every time we look, we notice, more and more are being added to do the work, but we can't seem to fathom why they are getting the same blessings as we are. It took you 20 years to get where you are and you really can't understand and you really don't want to accept that someone who just became a part of the body of Christ can come in working miracles and doing great exploits.

Matthew 20:9-15 NLT

⁹ When those hired at five o'clock were paid, each received a full day's wage. ¹⁰ When those hired first came to get their pay, they assumed they would receive more. But they, too, were paid a day's wage. ¹¹ When they received their pay, they protested to the owner, ¹² 'Those people worked only one hour, and yet you've paid them just as much as you paid us who worked all day in the scorching heat.'

¹³ "He answered one of them, 'Friend, I haven't been unfair! Didn't you agree to work all day for the usual wage? ¹⁴ Take your money and go. I wanted to pay this last worker the same as you. ¹⁵ Is it against the law for me to do what I want with my money? Should you be jealous because I am kind to others?'

We as the body of Christ, have really underestimated the kindness of God. We have not understood the depths of His kindness. We have become so conformed to the ways of this world that we've put Him in a box. How many of us assume we should receive more than others and we literally become indignant when we see others receiving the same? Has God not been good to you? Has He not given what He has promised?

We are living in the time of **A Full Day's Wage!** It shall be given even to those who have just come in. Will you co-operate with what God is doing? Don't limit His kindness.

The body of Christ is in an hour where we really can't afford not to receive all that God wants to give us, so that we can stand and overtake. We need the **fullness** of all that He wants to do and give. If He is willing and He is for us, we have to stop setting ourselves against each other.

Don't be anxious or jealous when those who came in last begin to prosper. God has more than enough and you will receive all that He has for you. No one else will be given "your" portion.

Please take heed to the question posed at the end of verse 15, "Should you be jealous because I am kind to others?"

4

ALLIES OF JEALOUSY

Declaration: No more open doors! Everything gets uprooted and destroyed!

It is no secret that the enemy doesn't fight alone. We see it over and over in Scripture in how kings continuously joined forces to come against the people of God. More often than not, there is always a hidden posse. There are demonic spirits that serve as door openers for other spirits.

Luke 11:24-26 NKJV

[24] "When an unclean spirit goes out of a man, he goes through dry places, seeking rest; and finding none, he says, 'I will return to my house from which I came.' [25] And when he comes, he finds it swept and put in order. [26] Then he goes and takes with him seven other spirits more

wicked than himself, and they enter and dwell there; and the last state of that man is worse than the first."

They will work together, recognizing and even honoring rank because their goal is your destruction, by any means necessary.

Joel 2:7-8 NLT
7 The attackers march like warriors
    and scale city walls like soldiers.
Straight forward they march,
    never breaking rank.
8 They never jostle each other;
    each moves in exactly the right position.
They break through defenses
    without missing a step.

How is it that demons and pure evil can work together so well that you would have a spirit standing in the gap and holding open the door for seven other spirits stronger than itself to come in and destroy a person? However, we in the body of Christ cannot come together and work together in much the same way? Contrarily, as soon as we see a person or persons stronger than we are, we shut the door, shut it down and send them away.

Why are we unable to move in exactly the right position—the position God has given us? Why do we refuse to let others move in the position God put them in without any dissension on our part?

As soon as we recognize that someone is anointed, we don't want anything to do with them. We want to be the strongest, we want to be the best, and we want to be the most anointed. As soon as we feel threatened by someone else being strong in the Lord, we attempt to sow seeds of discord and create division.

The word says there are six things the Lord hates, yes seven that are an abomination to Him and one of those things are those who sow seeds of discord in families. Are we not the family of God? Does not each one of us have a part and a place in the family of God? How can two walk together except they agree?

You say you want the Kingdom of Heaven advanced, but as soon as you see someone else doing their part to advance the Kingdom, you are no longer in agreement. If the kingdom of darkness can join forces to fulfill their plans and purposes in the earth, how much more should we be able to join forces? If a demon can open the door for seven demons stronger than it, how much more should we open the door for seven of our brothers and sisters in Christ Jesus who are strong in the Lord to come in and do the work that needs to be done?

We can NOT be a Kingdom set against itself; we can't afford to be divided. We know the Bible tells us that a kingdom set against or divided against itself can not stand. We also know that God tells us to do all that we can so that in the end we can remain standing.

Ephesians 6:12-13 NKJV

[12] For we do not wrestle against flesh and blood, but against principalities, against powers, against the rulers of the darkness of this age, against spiritual hosts of wickedness in the heavenly places. [13] Therefore take up the whole armor of God, that you may be able to withstand in the evil day, and having done all, to stand.

We need each other! We need our brothers and sisters in Christ to be able to stand. It's the enemy that we don't want to be so strong and united against us—we want our enemies to be scattered. Let God scatter our enemies so completely that no two of them will be able to come together and unite against us.

1 Samuel 11:11 NLT

But before dawn the next morning, Saul arrived, having divided his army into three detachments. He launched a surprise attack against the Ammonites and slaughtered them the whole morning. The remnant of their army was so badly scattered that no two of them were left together.

THEY THAT COME TOGETHER

What are some of these demonic allies that stand with the spirit of jealousy? The truth is, we sometimes are perplexed when jealousy rears its ugly head about "how" it happened—because we love God and we genuinely want to be right and do right. We make a practice of asking God to cleanse us from all unrighteousness, to search us and know us and see if there is any wicked way in us. We confess our sins, we pray for a sound mind and a restored soul. Yet, to our amazement, we can't seem to figure out how and why that spirit of jealousy was able to make an appearance and touch us. You have no idea why jealousy is having an effect on you and causing you to behave unbecomingly.

You have no idea that there are other spirits at work in your life that will open the door or keep open a door that has been there for some time. You seemed to be without transgression in this area for a while, but out of nowhere, here it is stirring up trouble. Baffled, you ask, "Where did you come from?" Little did you know, that crafty little spirit decided that it would return at a more "opportune time"—when things are going well in a relationship, when someone experiences sudden success and expects you to be happy for them, but you cannot. The only thing you can think of is why them and not me. When someone stumbles and falls and they reach out for your support and something on the inside of you feels gratified. When someone experiences hardships and trials, you find that you've been looking forward to the moment when finally everything isn't going well for them.

We know when it comes to deliverance and being totally set free, we have to get to the root of a matter and destroy everything connected to the very thing trying to destroy us. There were many times that God told His people and kings to utterly destroy their enemies—make no treaties and make no agreements.

Some of us have been bamboozled by the allies of jealousy as if they were protecting us or on our side. We've walked in agreement with some of them for years and it's time to part ways and say, "Good-bye insecurity, good-bye inferiority, good-bye low self-esteem, good-bye intimidation, good-bye pride—you will no longer be an open door to jealousy!"

These allies will come of no surprise to you; however, their covert operations may be so cunning that it can be undetectable to one who is not sober.

o Pride	o Fear of Rejection
o Fear	o Bitterness
o Insecurity	o Offense
o Inferiority	o Resentment
o Low Self-Esteem	o Orphan spirit
o Intimidation	o Self-Centeredness

✳ Pride

The interesting thing about pride is that it can create both passive and aggressive spiritual hostility. It can be both subtle and abrasive, hidden and obtrusive. Pride is the root cause of many evils and there is no surprise that it partners itself with a spirit of jealousy.

Proverbs 16:17-19 NLT
17 The path of the virtuous leads away from evil;
   whoever follows that path is safe.
18 Pride goes before destruction,
   and haughtiness before a fall.
19 Better to live humbly with the poor
   than to share plunder with the proud.

A spirit of pride in you can arouse a spirit of jealousy and insecurity in others.

Creating safe, welcome, non-toxic environments where people can learn where they are, grow, flourish and prosper is critical in this hour. All too often, we see many who are full of pride and they continuously boast about how anointed they are. They think more highly of themselves than they ought to and they eagerly let you know their position, title, rank, gifts and how they flow in the Spirit. They put themselves above you and position you beneath them.

Pride taints the atmosphere and creates an environment where the family of God begins to compete, compare and perform. Some are exalted and others are brought down low. There are many who have not yet come to a full understanding of who they are and what they are called to do in the body of Christ. When they enter into these environments full of pride, they shrink and feel as though they mind as well sit down somewhere, when in actuality they need the support of their brothers and sisters to help them stand and rise to carry out and fulfill the call on their lives. The novice is needed to come into maturity and the mature are needed to support, to teach, to train, to mentor, to cover, to guard, and to protect—not to gloat, offend and cause those who are being raised up to stumble and fall.

THE TODDLER EFFECT

Do you share or do you hoard? Do you invite or do you exclude?

Some of us have been like toddlers when it comes to the giftings and anointings God has given us.

When a toddler is playing with his toys, he would guard or hoard over them. The minute he sees another toddler showing interest, he doesn't hesitate to tell him, "No... mine!" Have you ever seen a teasing toddler—one who would get the attention of another just to tell him no?

We've seen many who have boasted about how gifted and anointed they are. They willingly shared encounters and stories of their relationship with God and exalted themselves instead of Jesus. As a result, others have felt rejected, abandoned, and left out of what was made to be an elite club for the "chosen." Instead of sharing the heart of the Father to extend an invitation for others to join in, they had the heart of a toddler, "This is only for me; this is mine."

On the other hand, to our credit, there have been those who humbly and graciously shared their relationship and the experiences they've had with God. It was their privilege and honor to let you know that you too can enter into the joy of the Lord and have the same—an intimate relationship with God. No, it may not look identical, but it will be your very own and it will be beautiful.

We don't have to be like the odd kid out on the sidelines watching others play. We don't have to be in the outer courts drooling over the inner court experiences of others.

We are children of the Most High God! His comfort is for us. The banquet is for us, and His goodness is for us. The Kingdom of Heaven is for all of God's sons and daughters.

If you've been in a place where you've been longingly observing God's goodness displayed in the lives of others, I encourage you—put down the binoculars. Come boldly into the presence of God, for a new and living way has been made for YOU through the body of Jesus Christ. Hallelujah!

HUMILITY CREATES SAFE PLACES

When I was coming into the knowledge of who I was and endeavoring to learn, I'd been in environments where I didn't feel good enough. Compared to how "anointed" others considered themselves or how "anointed" I considered them, I felt like I didn't measure up. There was never any doubt about their anointing, but every time I was around them, I struggled with insecurity. Now, you may say, it's not my fault that people are insecure or ask why should I have to water down my anointing to make others feel comfortable? Let me answer: No, it's not your fault others are insecure. Wouldn't you rather contribute to someone's prosperity and not their pain; to their strengths and not their struggles? You don't have to water down your anointing, but isn't it wonderful to come alongside someone and help them to recognize their anointing, so the Kingdom of God can advance, as many are better than one?

I've also had the privilege of being in the company of anointed vessels of God who were so very humble and it was such a breath of fresh air. It did not carry the stench of pride present in other environments. There was freedom and encouragement. It was safe and comforting and not hostile.

I can't emphasize enough the importance of walking in love and letting our hearts be filled with the faith and the love that comes with Christ Jesus.

We want to help people and not hurt people as we minister with the Lord. Others should feel the love of Christ, they should feel accepted and not rejected, they should feel included and not excluded, they should feel the love of God so strongly that they feel an invitation to be used by God just as you are being used by God. They should feel as though God wants to use them too instead of feeling like they are of no use. Yes, we do have a responsibility to humble ourselves under the mighty hand of God, let Him love through us and exalt the name of Jesus not ourselves.

Character is everything. We want to make sure we are operating in the fruit of the Spirit and not just taking the gifts and creating superiority or elitism.

Remember we are focusing on jealousy here. We don't want to be the ones responsible for causing one of our brothers and sisters to fall into this pit. You might ask, is the responsibility really on me? Well when it came to offense, Jesus said woe to the one who causes another to stumble. However, ultimately, yes, it was up to me to come out of agreement with insecurity and walk in the love of God.

2 Corinthians 6:3 NLT

We live in such a way that no one will stumble because of us, and no one will find fault with our ministry.

Know this, love makes it very difficult to be overtaken by jealousy. When we see an anointed person, who is full of love, kindness and humility, we don't want to be jealous of them, we want to support and celebrate with them. On the other hand, there are those who are anointed, full of pride and haughtiness. Let me tell you, people feel the total opposite of wanting to support them in this state.

You may not feel responsible or accountable, but you should ask yourself this, "Did my love fail or did my love prevail?" Remember without love you are a clanging cymbal.

There are some with wonderful ministries and sincere hearts.

2 Corinthians 5:12 NLT

Are we commending ourselves to you again? No, we are giving you a reason to be proud of us, so you can answer those who brag about having a spectacular ministry rather than having a sincere heart.

Understand your fearful responsibility to the Lord as Paul did and check your heart before standing before His people.

✳ Fear

I hate fear! Really, I do! Nothing has been more life-robbing. Uggghhh! When we think of the enemy who comes to steal, kill and destroy, it is easy to see how fear can be used as a weapon against us.

What has immobilized the body of Christ more? Time and time again, God tells us not to be afraid—to fear not. Do you remember when God was gathering Gideon's army and the ones who were afraid had to be released?

Have you ever been excluded (more often than not, excluding yourself) because you were afraid? Have you ever been robbed of a victory because you had fear? It kind of sucks to be released and counted out because you are scared, right? You'd much rather be as a fearless warrior who goes forth, knowing that if God is for you no one can be against you—knowing it is impossible to lose.

There are so many different types of fears, it's ridiculous. One thing we know for sure is that it is written in no uncertain terms, God has not given us a spirit of fear.

I'm encouraged by David who cried out to the Lord and God delivered him from ALL of his fears. ALL, every last one of them. Psalm 34:4

If you've ever felt imprisoned to a spirit of fear, be of good courage, it can be overcome. David wasn't delivered from ALL of his fears all at once. It was a process.

You don't have to fear that you won't measure up. You don't have to fear that God won't show up for you. You don't have to fear being the least of them. You don't have to fear being rejected.

F.E.A.R. = Forgetting Everything Already Reassured

God has already told us we don't have to fear or be discouraged. He assured us that He is with us, He will never leave us nor forsake us. He promised to help us and to uphold us with His victorious right hand. He promised to bring us through the floods and the fire unharmed. He promised to lead us in the paths of righteousness, to prepare a table before us in the presence of our enemies, to be our shield and our buckler, to be an ever-present help in our time of need and the promises go on and on.

It's time to command our souls...

Psalm 103:2 NKJV
Bless the LORD, O my soul,
And forget not all His benefits:

God LOVES us! His love is unfailing—despite how we feel, despite what we see, despite what comes against us, God will deliver us!

✳ Insecurity

Have you ever had a sinking feeling that you accepted less than what you are worth, yet at the same time you didn't feel worthy enough to demand more?

How's that for a dichotomy?

Have you ever felt like you had to take what you can get because there may not be another opportunity?

Have you ever been in a place where you gave so much, but received so little and neither party involved (this includes yourself) recognized the value of what you gave?

Have you ever discounted what you did or put a question mark after everything you said, because you get taunted with the accusation, "Who do you think you are?" Time and time again, you have failed to show up with the right level of boldness or the proper authority. You didn't show up as the competent leader or the knowledgeable expert.

Have you ever sat idly by while a confident go-getter confidently gave the wrong answer, and you knowing the right answer, were too insecure to speak up for fear that you "may" be wrong, even though you are right?

Have you ever stood by and watched something get poorly executed when deep down inside you know you have what it takes to do it with excellence? You were afraid to fail, mess up, look stupid, or get embarrassed? So, even though you're there, things never mount to the fullest potential because you fail to operate in your full potential.

Have you ever found yourself jealous of the one who was that confident go-getter—the one who dared to do all the things you wish you had the courage to do? They always ended up in the right places, making the right connections, getting these grand opportunities, then there's you—you end up in the same places to witness, but you never end up with the same results.

Uh yeah, I know—I'm over it too!

✳ Inferiority

Have you ever heard of the term, "Inferiority Complex?" I like to make use of definitions because oftentimes, we know what things mean in context, but when we read the definitions, we are stunned by how a word or term is defined. Definitions bring clarity and a deeper understanding. When I looked up the meaning of inferiority complex, I shook my head at what I read.

Here are two definitions I want to share and expound upon:

Bing (powered by Oxford Dictionaries)

- an unrealistic feeling of general inadequacy caused by actual or supposed inferiority in one sphere, sometimes marked by aggressive behavior in compensation.[8]

Merriam-Webster

- an acute sense of personal inferiority often resulting either in timidity or through overcompensation in exaggerated aggressiveness.[9]

I can't express enough that the way we see ourselves has such an impact on our lives that it has the power to determine whether we become leaders or followers, whether we prosper or are impoverished (this can be spiritual impoverishment), whether we succeed or fail, whether we advance or die where we are, whether we lose the battle or gain the victory.

An inferiority complex can make you believe you are a grasshopper as you perceive others to be giants. With this mindset, you will not pursue what is rightfully yours.

There are grave consequences when you fail to see yourself as God does. Many of you are familiar with the biblical account of when the spies went into the land God had promised them.

Number 13:33 NKJV
There we saw the giants (the descendants of Anak came from the giants); and we were like grasshoppers in our own sight, and so we were in their sight."

As we take from the definitions, inferiority is unrealistic feelings of inadequacy that would either cause us to show up timid and afraid or overcompensate with unnecessary and exaggerated aggression.

What has caused you to feel inferior? To whom have you felt inferior? It's time to stop showing up as a grasshopper and to show up in greatness to possess the promises God has for you.

✳ Low Self-Esteem

In its simplest form low self-esteem is a low and poor estimation of yourself. It has similarities to inferiority, but with inferiority there is someone with whom to compare yourself. With low self-esteem, it doesn't require anyone else to be considered in the equation.

How many have allowed low self-esteem to keep them on the sidelines? How many didn't go for that higher paying job or that position with leadership responsibility? How many times did you have something to say, but you didn't speak up? How many times did you determine within yourself that what you had to say wasn't good enough and you remained silent? How many times did you feel what you had to offer wasn't good enough to present? How many times did you hear after it was too late, "Why didn't you say something or why didn't you do it?"

Uh oh—how many are in a place where you are dissatisfied with where you are because you simply failed to take the risks, to step out of your comfort zones, to try, to start, to go, to move, to do it? The end result being the frustrating feeling of "I know there is more, God please tell me there is more." The truth is, God has already shown you, but you were afraid because you didn't feel like you measured up.

The good news is, it's never too late to come out of agreement with low self-esteem as long as you are breathing.

So, take a nice deep breath and give yourself another chance.

✳ Intimidation

Oftentimes when we are intimidated by a person or a thing, we tend to draw inward in timidity. It causes us to shrink back, to retreat or to withdraw. I like what Proverbs says:

Proverbs 24:10 NLT
If you fail under pressure,
    your strength is too small.

How many of us have been exhibiting strength that is just too small? The passion translation says if you faint when under pressure, you have need of courage.

Has God not said be strong and of good courage? This command deals with your small strength and the lack of courage we've shown. We can't afford to be afraid of men and their faces. We can't continue to be intimidated by the greatness in which others have the courage to walk.

Keep in mind, the same strength and courage and power and might and authority you see your brothers and sisters in Christ walking in is the same that is available to you. We all have this same command and it is not an option:

"Have I not commanded you? Be strong and of good courage; do not be afraid, nor be dismayed, for the LORD your God is with you wherever you go." Joshua 1:9 NKJV

✷ Fear of rejection

Have you ever seen how a fear of being rejected will get in the way of resolving present harmful and painful issues? Have you ever been afraid to broach a subject because of how it would make you look? Have you ever been deterred from requesting prayer because of what others might think of you if they only knew? The issue of jealousy may have been one you didn't want others to know you struggled with. This is why I'm glad we're addressing this issue collectively.

A fear of rejection assumes that people will respond unfavorably toward you.

A fear of rejection causes you to put up false walls of security that will reject people before they reject you.

A fear of rejection will have you afraid to read the email, open the letter, answer the call, give the message, preach the Word, teach with authority, present the idea or to even show up.

A fear of rejection denies the real you and presents a version of us we think others might accept.

Some of us are just now coming into the true knowledge of who we are because the real us has been oppressed for so long, for fear of not being accepted. We are just now coming into the true knowledge of God's love for us that empowers us to be our truest selves. Some of us are just now gaining the courage to accept the fact that not everyone is going to accept us, but it has no bearing on who we are or who we are not. Some of us are now starting to live out what it means to be rooted in the love of Christ.

Some of us are just now determining within ourselves that we can no longer delay showing up with what God has given us and believing that it will do what He sent it to do and reach who He wants it to reach. What God has given us is necessary and can no longer be denied.

We are gaining a new level of freedom to live unhidden, unrejected and unrestricted.

✳ Bitterness

Oh bitterness—would you go already! Bitterness is so deeply rooted that it has the capacity to deceive the one who has been hurt or wronged. Bitterness will blind your eyes to the truth and harden your heart to love.

Merriam-Webster

- a deep-seated ill will.[10]

My goodness! Bitterness is the point where resentment and offense have taken a seat and determined they aren't going anywhere. Bitterness has lodged itself in your heart. It has become a burden to you and a threat to your overall health.

Acts 8:23 NLT
for I can see that you are full of bitter jealousy and are held captive by sin."

Ephesians 4:31 NLT
Get rid of all bitterness, rage, anger, harsh words, and slander, as well as all types of evil behavior.

Hebrews 12:15 NLT
Look after each other so that none of you fails to receive the grace of God. Watch out that no poisonous root of bitterness grows up to trouble you, corrupting many.

✳ Offense

Proverbs 19:11 ESV
Good sense makes one slow to anger,
    and it is his glory to overlook an offense.

Earlier on, I mentioned that sometimes our very own ill-placed expectations create disappointment and open the door to offense. I really think this was worth repeating.

Be careful with offense. It is a snare and a trap. When we operate in offense, it sometimes, deceivingly looks like the other person is getting the short end of the stick in our offense, but we don't realize it is actually us receiving the short end until it is too late.

As you've read, being easily offended is one of the manifestations of jealousy. We become easily offended by those of whom we are jealous.

Here is something else I want you to pay attention to—jealousy would actually cause you to be offended by someone else being great. We actually demand of them within ourselves, "Who are you?" "Who do you think you are?" "Who gave you the authority?" "Who put you in charge?" "Who made you an expert?" "Did God really tell you that?" Uh oh! We want to really begin to walk circumspectly and tread lightly. Did not Satan and the Pharisees pose and ponder these same questions concerning Jesus? We don't want to operate in these spirits.

✳ Resentment

Make sure you don't resent God for what He's doing in someone's life by not believing He will do it for you or is going to do it for you.

Job 5:2 NLT
Surely resentment destroys the fool,
    and jealousy kills the simple.

Here again, we see resentment as one of those self-destructing attitudes and spirits that proves more harmful to oneself than to others. Be careful with this one because as with offense, this spirit hides behind self-justification; whereby, you may feel justified due to someone else's behavior or action.

Many are familiar with resentment because they have walked in it at one time or another, for one reason or another. There are many who resented decisions they've made and how things turned out.

Resentment is bitter indignation at having been treated unfairly[1]. Now when it comes to "being treated unfairly," this can be both true and perceived. This is why I say to be careful you don't resent God for what He's doing for others. There can be a perceived unfairness—which in essence is saying that God is doing things unjustly and this is impossible with God.

You don't have to waste another moment resenting anything or anyone because our God is a Redeemer!

Genesis 50:20 NLT
You intended to harm me, but God intended it all for good. He brought me to this position so I could save the lives of many people.

Don't fret, God can turn around everything that was meant to work against you, to put you in a position where He can work through you.

✳ Orphan Spirit

Psalm 84:11 NLT
For the LORD God is our sun and our shield.
   He gives us grace and glory.
The LORD will withhold no good thing
   from those who do what is right.

Have you ever read about, heard about or seen live in action someone's personal, intimate relationship with God? Have you seen someone operating in the gifts of the Holy Spirit, demonstrating the power of God, praying powerfully, healing the sick, working miracles, prophesying on a high level, or seeing in the spiritual realm through dreams and visions?

Now, the desire you already have to know God more, to hear His voice clearer, and to do great things, is even more aroused. All of a sudden, you're having these thoughts (though it may not be the first time), that it's easier for everyone else, and it seems like everybody and their momma are doing great things, except for you. You feel left out and not as valuable or significant. You take it up with God and ask a bunch of whys and whens. Then, you reluctantly conclude that maybe you need to pray more, fast more, or read the Word more. You think about the possible sins that might be hindering you.

Yes, that orphan spirit will make you think you have to do more, perform better, and sin less, because after all you're not totally approved or somehow don't quite make the mark.

WHAT ABOUT MY PARTY?

I think it's very interesting how in the account of the prodigal son, neither the prodigal nor his older brother really understood the love of the father. Their behavior reminds me of some of the characteristics of those with an orphan spirit would sometimes exhibit. There was greater value placed on what they did either to lose or to earn their father's love, than on his love itself.

The prodigal son thought since he sinned against God and his father, he was no longer "worthy" to be called his son. His older brother thought he should have received his love and special recognition because of how hard he worked for him.

We must realize that God's love can't be lost and it can't be earned. He has always loved us with a love that doesn't change nor does it fail.

Have you ever had a difficult time celebrating someone receiving God's love in a way you thought you worked hard to receive? As I mentioned before, sometimes it's hard to celebrate someone just saved and working miracles while you've been serving and doing the work of the Lord for 20 years and still believing for certain manifestations of God to break forth in your ministry or in your walk with Him. Where's your party, right?

Luke 15:20-32 NIV
20 So he got up and went to his father.
"But while he was still a long way off, his father saw him and was filled with compassion for him; he ran to his son, threw his arms around him and kissed him.
21 "The son said to him, 'Father, I have sinned against heaven and against you. I am no longer worthy to be called your son.'
22 "But the father said to his servants, 'Quick! Bring the best robe and put it on him. Put a ring on his finger and sandals on his feet. 23 Bring the fattened calf and kill it. Let's have a feast and celebrate. 24 For this son of mine

was dead and is alive again; he was lost and is found.' So they began to celebrate.

²⁵ "Meanwhile, the older son was in the field. When he came near the house, he heard music and dancing. ²⁶ So he called one of the servants and asked him what was going on. ²⁷ 'Your brother has come,' he replied, 'and your father has killed the fattened calf because he has him back safe and sound.'

²⁸ "The older brother became angry and refused to go in. So his father went out and pleaded with him. ²⁹ But he answered his father, 'Look! All these years I've been slaving for you and never disobeyed your orders. Yet you never gave me even a young goat so I could celebrate with my friends. ³⁰ But when this son of yours who has squandered your property with prostitutes comes home, you kill the fattened calf for him!'

³¹ "'My son,' the father said, 'you are always with me, and everything I have is yours. ³² But we had to celebrate and be glad, because this brother of yours was dead and is alive again; he was lost and is found.'"

Can you just feel the love of God in these passages? While the prodigal son was afar off, his father ran to him ready to embrace him and welcome him back home. His return was worth celebrating, him being found alive was worth celebrating. It didn't matter what he did as his sins weren't being held against him or preventing him from accessing the father. The father's love was enough to cover his sins, to forgive him and to restore him to his rightful place as a son. As for the one who was faithful, why couldn't he see that everything the father had was already his to share in?

Those with an orphan spirit have not yet come to the understanding of God's love for them. Yes, they can quote all the Scriptures about it, but they have not sunk deep down into their hearts. This unfailing love somehow seems to elude them, yet they can see it expressed and poured out on everyone else so easily.

May you truly connect with the heart of God, our Father. May you know the width, the length, the height and the depth of His love for you by experience so that you would be complete in Him. Nothing can ever separate you from God's love. Be free in Him.

✳ Self-centeredness

Philippians 2:1-5 NLT

Is there any encouragement from belonging to Christ? Any comfort from his love? Any fellowship together in the Spirit? Are your hearts tender and compassionate? ² Then make me truly happy by agreeing wholeheartedly with each other, loving one another, and working together with one mind and purpose.

³ Don't be selfish; don't try to impress others. Be humble, thinking of others as better than yourselves. ⁴ Don't

look out only for your own interests, but take an interest in others, too.

⁵ You must have the same attitude that Christ Jesus had.

My goodness! This scripture here far surpasses anything I could have thought to address under self-centeredness. It is literally all in His Word. Please go back and read it carefully with the lens of how the spirit of jealousy works with self-centeredness. I think the solution is all in this scripture. Carefully ponder the questions posed:

1. Are you encouraged simply because you belong to Christ?
2. Do you find comfort from God's love?
3. Is there true fellowship in the Spirit?
4. Is your heart tender and compassionate? No...for real! Is your heart tender and compassionate?
5. Do you wholeheartedly agree with others in Christ or only when it benefits you in some way?
6. Do you truly love your brothers and sisters in Christ? Do you truly love her? Do you truly love him? You know who they are—put their name in the question. The one you've been struggling with jealousy towards. Ask yourself, "Do I truly love [Michelle]?"
7. Am I able to work well with others with one mind and one purpose or is it my way or the highway?
8. Are you selfish or exhibit selfish tendencies?

9. Have you found yourself trying to impress others?
10. Are you humble?
11. Do you generally look out for your own interests or do you genuinely take an interest in others too?
12. Do you have the same attitude that Christ had?

You might want to go and read the remaining verses in chapter 2 of Philippians.

It's time to get over ourselves and truly walk in love to advance the Kingdom of Heaven. We have to recognize when we are getting in the way. We have to recognize when our selfish ambition and motives are getting in the way of God's will being done on earth as it is in Heaven. We have to recognize when our unwillingness to love, to forgive, to support, to encourage, or to pray, is getting in the way.

We have to recognize when leaning on our own understanding is taking us in the wrong direction, causing division and giving strength to our enemies.

5

DON'T TAKE THE BAIT

Declaration: I will not be ensnared by the traps of the enemy—they shall remain empty!

Psalm 119:133 NKJV
Direct my steps by Your word,
And let no iniquity have dominion over me.

BE CAREFUL WHAT FLAMES YOU FAN—WHEN THE FIRE SPREADS YOU MIGHT GET BURNED

Have you ever played into something or entertained something negative you wish you hadn't? While in the moment, you felt justified when you played into it or were just being haughty or petty. You had no idea that after it was all said and done, you would come out wounded, with your feelings hurt and looking like the bad guy—totally in the wrong and regretting it. Don't take the bait!

SOCIAL MEDIA FRENZY

So you heard about, read about, saw a social media post about how those who were considered the unlikely or least likely, now having a thriving business, a thriving ministry or a thriving relationship, etc. You thought it was cool and you were even intrigued, but if we're being honest and exposing jealousy, there was a crack in your door that wanted to continue chatting about it, reading about it or scrolling in hopes to find something negative.

Oftentimes we offer ourselves a false sense of peace and comfort by assuaging that jealous spirit with statements like, "All that glitters isn't gold," "The grass isn't always greener on the other side," "It's not always what it's cracked up to be," "People will only show you what they want you to see," etc., then you go on about your business, slightly recognizing that what just transpired within you wasn't quite right.

What actually took place was one manifestation of jealousy, covering like a blanket, another manifestation of a different form or fashion. It only disguises the smoke, at best, when in reality there is still a fire that needs to be quenched.

Sometimes we can look at someone else's fruit tree and suddenly become hungry. This is a great example of what jealousy is, it arouses in you feelings of discontentment. You see a tree in full bloom and then look at your own and perceive dry branches or scarcity. You may fail to realize, to everything there is a season, a time for every purpose under heaven. The truth is, that person you're looking at may be in their spring or summer season and you may be in winter. Winter is not bad, it's simply your time to nourish what had been planted so that when your appointed time comes you can yield a bountiful harvest. There will always be seed, time and harvest. The time in between the seed and harvest may vary, being shorter or longer; however, we are so grateful that God gives seed to the sower and He has your harvest in mind.

So, before you begin the examination and comparison process of someone else's fruit, stop and say, "I too am an oak of righteousness, the planting of the Lord for His glory and I shall be fruitful and multiply!"

AN EXPOSÉ OF YOUR HEART

Jealousy exposes and feeds off the condition of your heart and your mind. It feeds off of your lack of knowledge or understanding. It feeds off of your lack of truth. In other words, jealousy thrives in dead places of lack, insufficiency, misguided hopes, desires and lies.

One of the prevailing thoughts that enters your mind is, "he's better than me or she's better than me." You feel like they're more gifted, more anointed, more talented, more skilled, smarter, or more attractive. To sum it up, you feel like they are in a better position than you are.

Listen, I know that the phrase "better than me" may sound a little trivial and immature—but let's face it, even as children we've had uncomfortable and painful run-ins with this very matter. Some of you may even see it in your own children. Little Johnny was sad because he felt like everybody on the basketball team did "better than him." Little Susie was a little discouraged because she felt like everybody in her class did "better than her" in the spelling bee. I'm sure as an adult you can think of a few instances in your adulthood when you felt like everybody did "better than you" and you were bothered by it. If it wasn't "everybody," it was "somebody" you felt did better than you and you were a little irritated.

Even the things that may seem childish can be effective tools for the enemy to use against us, if we allow it.

When you see your brothers and sisters in Christ, when you see others in your work place, in your family, wherever you are, what comes to your mind? If they are pretty, if they are handsome, good looking, if they appear happy, if they appear successful, if they appear powerful, if they appear to be accepted, if they appear to be pre-ferred, if they appear to be a person of influence, if others flock to them, what comes to your mind? What thoughts do you have? What emotions do you feel?

I challenge you to let the Holy Spirit transform you into a new person by the way you think and subsequently and intentionally, let your actions follow suit.

When you see people, begin to thank the Lord for them. Thank the Lord for who they are. Thank the Lord for the gifts He has given them. Thank the Lord for strength-ening them. Thank the Lord for accomplishing His pur-pose in them and through them. Thank the Lord for using them to advance His Kingdom. Thank the Lord for the glory He will receive from them. Thank the Lord for bless-ing them. Thank the Lord for helping them. Thank the Lord for providing for them. Thank the Lord for encourag-ing them. Thank the Lord for His love for them. Thank the Lord for their salvation.

If you feel tempted to watch somebody's life—to watch to see what achievements they make, what doors open for them, who's supporting them, how much they're advanc-ing, and all the while you're hoping they're not getting too far ahead of you—stop, pull the plug and remember that your times are in God's hands.

BE SOBER AND BE VIGILANT

In these times, we really have to be careful to guard our hearts with all diligence. We have to recognize and understand that words are seed carriers looking to be planted. There are words we want to take root and grow and there are words we want to fall to the ground. Be careful, sometimes the words and actions of others, including those you trust, can carry with it the seeds of jealousy. If you notice, after a person has said or done a particular thing, you began struggling with jealous thoughts and it literally feels like warfare in your mind and your emotions as you battle not to be overtaken.

It's not so much the person, as it is the assignment of what the words or actions were sent to do. Abort the seeds and curse them at the root so they won't grow and bear fruit. Do not water them! Do not ignore them! Kill them!

LOVE WITHOUT HYPOCRISY

Romans 12:9-13 NLT

9 Don't just pretend to love others. Really love them. Hate what is wrong. Hold tightly to what is good. 10 Love each other with genuine affection, and take delight in honoring each other. 11 Never be lazy, but work hard and serve the Lord enthusiastically. 12 Rejoice in our confident

hope. Be patient in trouble, and keep on praying. [13] When God's people are in need, be ready to help them. Always be eager to practice hospitality.

There is now a popular meme, "Fix your sisters crown without letting the world know it's crooked."

We really have to be serious about loving each other with pure hearts and without hypocrisy. In this hour, we can't afford to keep pretending to love and care—we really have to love and care. Check your heart. If you feel a desire to let others know about someone's short-comings, their flaws, their mistakes, or their weaknesses, then make sure you don't put yourself in a position to gain access to their vulnerabilities. If you are not mature and healthy enough spiritually, mentally and emotionally to be trusted with this knowledge, you may not be ready to be granted access.

When you are given access, this is where you get to love without hypocrisy. If you are close enough to fix her crown and be used by God, don't let jealousy taint or destroy such a beautiful thing. It's a privilege and an honor to be close enough to the person to fix the crown and at the same time be close enough to God's heart to love them through it...without hypocrisy.

What does it look like to fix your sister's crown without letting the world know it's crooked? It looks very much like things that are done behind the scenes. It's not shouting from the rooftops about what you've done, it's not looking for recognition or praise, it's not looking to build your reputation or your resume, and it's not seeking to build your platform. It is in your prayer closet, when it's just you and God, lifting them up and pleading for them in prayer. It's inquiring about how you can be of help to them from a pure heart, it's offering practical assistance, or perhaps even love offerings of financial support. Fixing someone's crown may not be seen as a glamorous position, but it is however, one of humility, honor and love.

REJOICE

God is a generous gift giver!

One day, my son interrupted my study time. He was super excited to show me the new toy his father gave him. He is an only child and has so many toys, but every time he receives a new toy, it still excites him. What he had already been given has no bearing or puts no damper on him being just as excited to welcome something new.

I thought, "Wow, he already has so many toys and yet he continues to be showered with gifts." I immediately thought about God and how generous He is. He doesn't withhold any good thing from us. He doesn't look at us and think He already gave us a gift and will therefore give us no more. He actually delights in our prosperity. He loves to bless us and show us His loving-kindness.

The nature of God is to pour out: He pours out His Spirit; He opens the windows of Heaven and pours out blessings we don't have room enough to receive. He gives wisdom generously and without reproach. He makes rivers to flow out of our bellies...RIVERS! He causes it to rain on the just and the unjust...RAIN! There are so many examples that could be given.

It's time to get use to the outpouring! Not just get used to it, but believe for it, hope for it, pray for it, embrace it, celebrate it and glorify your Father in Heaven for it—not just for yourself but for others. Don't shrink back overcome with jealousy, REJOICE! Give God His glory! When your sister is rejoicing over yet another blessing and yet another miracle, REJOICE! In this season, we dare not count another's blessings and wonder why God is blessing her AGAIN.

Remember it is the nature of our God to bless us. He is just, righteous, and faithful. He is the same yesterday, today and forevermore. So, guess what He's going to do? Continue to bless us! Jealousy won't stop Him! I suggest we come out of agreement with that spirit, repent and take joy in the Kingdom of Heaven for which a place has been made for us in God's family. No more seeds of discord and division. It's time to unite! It's time to support each other like never before because the blessings are pouring out like never before. Your sisters can't carry alone all that God is releasing in this hour. It's going to be bountiful and you are included!

DON'T LET JEALOUSY BE AGAINST YOU

Revelation 2:20 NKJV

Nevertheless I have a few things against you, because you allow that woman Jezebel, who calls herself a prophetess, to teach and seduce My servants to commit sexual immorality and eat things sacrificed to idols.

Can you imagine hearing Jesus Himself say to you that He has a few things "against" you? I can imagine you'd be like Sanford Simpson dramatically holding his heart. I can imagine you'd much prefer to hear the first words out of Jesus' mouth, in verses 18b-19, stating what He loves about you and of what He approves: "'These things says the Son of God, who has eyes like a flame of fire, and His feet like fine brass: [19] "I know your works, love, service, faith, and your patience; and as for your works, the last are more than the first."

Who wants to hear, "Nevertheless" after that! I'm not saying we will never fall short or make mistakes. I absolutely love being corrected by God—there is no shame or condemnation—there's gratefulness for His love toward us that He would take the time to lovingly correct us when we are in error.

When I thought about how the people of Thyatira tolerated Jezebel, it made me think about how the people of God today tolerate jealousy.

We've felt it many times, but we've tolerated it. We've experienced it many times, but we've tolerated it. We treated people certain ways as a result of it, but we tolerate it. Relationships were destroyed as a result of it, but we tolerate it. How long will we have this issue and not deal with it? How many relationships will be destroyed before we deal with it? How much damage needs to be done before we say **ENOUGH!**

6

LOOKING IN THE MIRROR

Declaration: By the grace of God I am what I am: and His grace which was bestowed upon me was not in vain; — 1 Corinthians 15:10

HAVE I LEARNED TO LOVE "ME"

When you consider "YOU," what do you think? What comes to mind? Are you satisfied? Are you in love? Are you ecstatic and filled with joy when you consider yourself: who you are, where you are, and where you're going and what you are growing into? Or on the other hand, are you a little disappointed when you ponder these questions? Are you discouraged? Are you upset, angry or bitter? Do you despise where you are? Are you dissatisfied with who you are?

Another question that is even more valid and critical—do you even know who you are? Is your identity solid? Now, I realize that at this point you can go off on a religious tangent. You can start thinking about all the Scriptures that speak about your identity in Christ, which of course we need to know. However, my concern is, we are adept at quoting, but we truthfully have not learned to live it. As a result, we can quote the Bible and make it sound wonderful, but the truth is, we are failing in the very same areas of these Scriptures we are religiously quoting.

The Pharisees knew the Scriptures, but they did not know the Life of the Word. They had the appearance, but they lacked the power. Such as it is with many of us today, we have the appearance and we can make it sound good and look good, but we are lacking. We are lacking in strength, lacking in faith, lacking in power, lacking in love, lacking in joy, lacking in peace, lacking in patience, lacking a sound mind, lacking in trusting God, lacking in healing and wholeness, lacking in deliverance, etc.

Do you absolutely, unequivocally, unashamedly LOVE YOU? Have you learned to love you? Did you learn how to embrace the **"Real"** you? Have you embraced your unique sound—your voice? Have you embraced your purpose, your calling, your assignment? Have you embraced the way you minister, the way you pray, the way you sing, the way you worship, the way you teach? We know there are differences in the administration of the gifts of the Spirit;

have you embraced how the Holy Spirit works with and through you? Have you embraced all of the good things that are on the inside of you in Christ that would make you effective as you share Christ, the Good News?

Philemon 1:6 NKJV
that the sharing of your faith may become effective by the acknowledgment of every good thing which is in you in Christ Jesus.

Have you acknowledged every good thing which is in you in Christ Jesus? Acknowledging according to Strong's Concordance is recognition, full discernment, (ac)knowledge(-ing, -ment)[11].

In other words, because I want to drive this home, do you have knowledge of all the good things God put on the inside of you? Have you fully discerned it? Have you recognized it? I ask this because we are talking about looking in the mirror. We are talking about overcoming jealousy.

Do you think if you had full knowledge, recognize completely and fully discern all the good things in you through Christ Jesus that jealousy would be stirred up when you see your brothers and sisters walking in the goodness of the Lord, walking in their calling and doing great things with God?

I can almost guarantee that if you had this knowledge, recognition and full discernment, you would also recognize that YOU LACK NO GOOD THING!

Let me ask you this: Is it possible to feel less than, inferior, intimidated, insecure, or unworthy if you truly understood who you are and what is in you?

If you were to fully embrace who you are and what you carry, with the knowledge that it is soooo good, because God didn't short change any of us, would you still be prone to falling prey to jealousy?

So, what now? I say, look in the mirror baby! What is in you is far greater than you can ask, think or imagine... it has never even entered your mind! However, the Holy Spirit is going to reveal it to you! You are about to walk in full discernment and recognition! In this season, you are about to acknowledge just who you are in Christ and it is going to be so GOOD!

Somebody say, "Goodbye jealousy! I will see you no more again FOREVER, in the Name of Jesus!"

WHO AM I – WHERE AM I

At this point, you should be hyped and excited. I am! We do however, want to keep things in perspective and walk this out circumspectly. It is difficult to overcome this spirit of jealousy if you don't know who you are and have a vision of where you are going! The battle will be constant as the enemy will continuously rear its ugly head. The enemy is always looking for a "more" opportune time.

Now when the devil had ended every temptation, he departed from Him until an opportune time. Luke 4:13 (NKJV). The KJV says, "he departed from him for a season." In his mind, the enemy thinks (I imagine in an Arnold Swarzeneggar voice), "I'll be back!" The question is: Will you be ready when he returns?

The enemy is tireless in his pursuit, he does not grow weary in trying to destroy you. He is dedicated and intentional in his objective, persistent in his hunt, and driven by his purpose—The thief does not come except to steal, and to kill, and to destroy. John 10:10 (NKJV)

Let us be diligent to spend time with the Lord so He can show us who we are and where He is taking us.

IT'S TIME TO DRAW THE CURTAINS

Let us be sober and put an end to the stage play we've been performing in. For some, you may be able to pinpoint the root of a jealous spirit because it started at home with your siblings. Your brother or sister was the favorite, they were smarter, they were more talented, etc. You've developed a performance-based acceptance model as a child that was built on COMPARE, COMPETE, and PERFORM. We have totally ignored or failed to recognize our gifts, talents and skills. We regard them as not being good enough, simply because we feel others have not recognized them.

So, our behavior oftentimes isn't organic to us. Instead, however, it is a response to someone else's gifts, talents and skills in which we try to convince ourselves, and others, that we can do that too—that we are just as good— that we are special too. As a result, we never learn who we really are or cultivate our unique factors because we spend our energy trying to keep up in spaces and places that were never ours.

We waste our time trying to be good at somebody else's life, somebody else's calling and somebody else's gifts and our very own are hidden and dying

---

And you wonder why your soul is crying out, the feeling of being unfulfilled is deepening and the pain of a broken heart from dreams unrecognized is eating you from the inside out. It is because the very thing God called you to do, you have despised, discounted and rejected because it didn't look like someone else's. You never got into the presence of the One who created you and knit you in your mother's womb to find out what He wants to do with the gifts He placed on the inside of you.

You can't forever ignore the truth that you are His masterpiece, His workmanship created for good works in Christ Jesus before the foundation of the world so that you can WALK in it (Ephesians 2:10). You were created to walk in your own purpose, gifts and talents. Your life is not your own. You were bought with a price.

What scale are you using to measure your success? It's time to draw the curtains!

OTHERS WILL SET THE STAGE FOR YOU

Get ready for this, because it is critical for you to understand so that you don't forfeit what God has given you. It's not a comparison or a competition. You simply must let others do their part. Let them set the stage, let them prepare the way. Why? There are some things God has for you that will require others to go before you to prepare the way. It is not a one-man show and it will require the work of our brothers and sisters in Christ to see the full spectrum of what God is trying to accomplish.

You don't have to do it all alone. Especially when it comes to the great exploits God wants to do with you—it may require the hearts of the people to be prepared. Don't be afraid that the greatness of others will cause you to be robbed. Don't get discouraged by how good another person preaches about, teaches about, talks about or does something about what God called you to do also. It doesn't matter who or how many are touching on the issue God called you to address. They are simply doing their part and you most come forth to do yours. God will sometimes use many vessels and it may look like the same message, but it doesn't make any person unnecessary. You are not the unnecessary person.

Here's a phenomenal example of what this looks like. Both John and Matthew shared the same message about the account of Jesus feeding the 5,000 and when He walked on water. Both accounts were recorded in the bible and both are necessary. They both have their own unique way of sharing the message and what you find in one account you don't find in the other and vice versa. For instance, Matthew's account of Jesus walking on the water shares the details of Peter stepping out of the boat to walk on the water toward Jesus, but John's account does not. John's account of Jesus feeding the 5,000 shares the extra details of how Jesus tested Philip, which I think is a very interesting dynamic. These extra details, in both cases, are such a blessing to us. Can you imagine if John would've said, "Well, Matthew already shared the message, so there's no need for me to share it too." Be encouraged to go forward with your part.

Understand that if God gave it to you, if He gave you the work, then it is for you. I will say this, pray about the time and the season—ask God when He wants this work completed. Ask God when He wants it to be released. Ask Him for the strategy and for His heart. Ask Him about the plan for the work He gave you—the work He prepared for you.

You don't want to be lackadaisical with the work He gave you. You don't want to be slow, nor do you want to be disobedient; we have to know His timing. We can't drag our feet thinking we can do it whenever we feel like it or whenever we get to it; we have to know the Lord's plan. On the other hand, you don't want to rush and release things prematurely because others are doing their part.

THINGS THAT MAKE YOU GO...HMMMM

Have you ever asked yourself: "Why am I jealous of 'certain' people while I can be genuinely happy for certain others with no envy at all?"

Why weren't you jealous when God moved mightily through Mr. Morrison or when Mrs. Mitchell worked a miracle?

Why didn't it bother you when God let little, 5-year-old, James, encounter Heaven in multiple visitations?

Why weren't you filled with envy when Jesus revealed Himself in a supernatural visitation to that woman in India or that man in China?

However, when God showed Veronica that vision you were beside yourself with jealousy. When God spoke to Lisa in a dream you were riddled with envy. When God used Maria to heal the sick, you were wondering why He didn't use you.

What is or was the difference? Why are you jealous of certain people, but are genuinely able to praise God for others?

Why do you feel threatened by Rachel, but are un-moved by Leah?

Why aren't you bothered when God uses Lois, but you can barely contain yourself when He starts using Sheila?

One thing that God makes perfectly clear is this: Man looks at the outward appearance, but He looks at the heart.

The outward appearance of a person or a situation can be dangerously deceiving. When we couple it with our own perception (which may not be true) and our own understanding (which may be severely lacking), an open door is given to figments of our imagination.

It is in this space that we become intimidated by Tiphany and threatened by Laura, but we will support others. Yet, unbeknownst to us, it is Tiphany and Laura who have the clean heart, although we "perceive" something different.

We, out of ignorance, compare ourselves to certain people when we're jealous. When we're not, we readily admit, "I have no reason to hate on so-and-so because I am not in competition with her." However, when jealousy is stirred, it does cause you to compare and even if only in your heart, you begin to compete and you begin to measure yourself up to them.

In other words, jealousy of "certain" people sometimes happens because you internally position yourself in a certain place (based on how you see yourself and what you think of yourself) and you internally position others (based on how you see them and what you think of them). When these internal positions conflict, your security is threatened and when you don't perceive any conflict, you feel safe. For example, there was no conflict when you measured yourself in comparison to your pastor. However, the internal positioning of yourself as compared to someone seemingly of your same "rank," position or status, created a conflict and you put more weight on outward appearance than you did the heart. You leaned unto your own understanding and expectations.

ESTEEM-MATION

The way we esteem ourselves and others play a huge part in our response towards other people. This is why you can be jealous of one person and not another. It is the level at which you esteem them, relative to your own self-esteem that causes such inner turmoil.

Esteem is the worth or value YOU place on a person or a thing.

Esteem is YOUR opinion or judgment of a person or a thing...uh oh—do you see where things can get twisted?

Esteem is what YOU think and what YOU believe—help us God because oftentimes, what we think and what we believe is not even the case.

Esteem is the regard in which YOU hold a person or a thing, be it in high esteem or low esteem.

Esteem = Estimation (YOUR Estimation)

Unhealthy patterns and behaviors that lead to jealousy and other divisions can come from the condition of your heart and mind, which can be unhealed and unsanctified.

Unhealthy	**Healthy**
Esteem them/yourself (estimation)	Love
Misperceptions	Truth
Lack of Understanding	Understanding
Need for God's Perspective	God's perspective
Need for God's Heart	God's Heart

A wrong perspective or a misperception can put a person with wickedness in their heart on a pedestal and a person with a pure heart, just trying to please God, as a pauper. Thus, when you see the one you wrongly esteemed as a pauper prospering, your heart can become set against them in jealousy, wondering why them and not you. Since pride and many other issues can play a part in the grand scheme of things, it is imperative to conduct a total heart check.

Love can overcome it all. There are two things to request of God that will bring peace, truth and a right response in a situation: (1) God what is your perspective? (2) God give me Your heart towards him/her and the situation?

Do not be overcome by evil, but overcome evil with good. Romans 12:21 NKJV

Romans 13:10-13 NLT

[10] Love does no wrong to others, so love fulfills the requirements of God's law. [11] This is all the more urgent, for you know how late it is; time is running out. Wake up, for

our salvation is nearer now than when we first believed. [12] The night is almost gone; the day of salvation will soon be here. So remove your dark deeds like dirty clothes, and put on the shining armor of right living. [13] Because we belong to the day, we must live decent lives for all to see. Don't participate in the darkness of wild parties and drunkenness, or in sexual promiscuity and immoral living, or in quarreling and jealousy.

Yes! It is time to remove jealousy like dirty clothes!

Wait! Did you catch that? Side nugget—right living is armor! I love that! Put it on!

Welcome your brothers and sisters in Christ and all that they do for the Lord.

Philippians 2:29-30 NLT
[29] Welcome him in the Lord's love and with great joy, and give him the honor that people like him deserve. [30] For he risked his life for the work of Christ, and he was at the point of death while doing for me what you couldn't do from far away.

Remember, we all have our place. You're in that city, in that country, at that church, in that ministry, and in that job, just so God can use you. He knew where you would be born and where you would live. Let people do and be what God needs them to do and be, while you do and be what God positioned you to do and be. Period! Everybody has a part and God graciously equips us to carry out the work.

Do you remember when David, the man after God's own heart, wanted to build a house for God? What did God tell him? God told him that he couldn't. He also told David why he couldn't and who He chose to build His house instead (1 Chronicles 28).

We have to recognize that although we may have it in our hearts to do certain things, we may not be called or chosen to do them. It has to be enough for us to know that what we want is being accomplished, even if it's not through us, because it is all about God.

When David found out he wasn't the set man for the assignment, he didn't behave unbecomingly. He did what any person with God's heart would do—he helped his son Solomon and gave him the blueprints. He stepped aside and let Solomon do his part—what he was called to do.

It wasn't that David wasn't good enough; we all know how God feels about David and David knew it too.

1 Chronicles 28:3-6 NLT

[3] but God said to me, 'You must not build a Temple to honor my name, for you are a warrior and have shed much blood.'

⁴ "Yet the LORD, the God of Israel, has chosen me from among all my father's family to be king over Israel forever. For he has chosen the tribe of Judah to rule, and from among the families of Judah he chose my father's family. And from among my father's sons the LORD was pleased to make me king over all Israel. ⁵ And from among my sons—for the LORD has given me many—he chose Solomon to succeed me on the throne of Israel and to rule over the LORD's kingdom. ⁶ He said to me, 'Your son Solomon will build my Temple and its courtyards, for I have chosen him as my son, and I will be his father.

Like David, when we know, beyond a shadow of doubt, what our part is and what we are called to do, we won't waste time being jealous or coveting another person's part—we have our own work to do. We likewise can't be jealous of the gifts that others walk in. We have to recognize that certain gifts are needed to accomplish the work God chose us to do and we want everyone to be well equipped to carry it out.

Just like every article in the temple was given a certain measure of gold or silver by weight depending on how each would be used, so it is with each part in the body of Christ. We are given certain or a measure of gifts, skills, talents, authority, mantles, etc. according to our call and purpose.

Therefore, recognize that our gifts may differ and our parts may differ, but we are still one body and we belong to each other.

Romans 12:3-8 NLT

[3] Because of the privilege and authority God has given me, I give each of you this warning: Don't think you are better than you really are. Be honest in your evaluation of yourselves, measuring yourselves by the faith God has given us. [4] Just as our bodies have many parts and each part has a special function, [5] so it is with Christ's body. We are many parts of one body, and we all belong to each other.

[6] In his grace, God has given us different gifts for doing certain things well. So if God has given you the ability to prophesy, speak out with as much faith as God has given you. [7] If your gift is serving others, serve them well. If you are a teacher, teach well. [8] If your gift is to encourage others, be encouraging. If it is giving, give generously. If God has given you leadership ability, take the responsibility seriously. And if you have a gift for showing kindness to others, do it gladly.

POM-POM MENTALITY

The good thing about God is He gives us everything we need to live a life that is pleasing to Him. He gives us everything we need to complete the work He prepared for us.

Imagine with me for a moment two young girls, sisters, both loved and talented. Monica has a love for cheerleading and Elizabeth loves playing the piano. The one who loves the piano hates cheerleading and the one who loves cheerleading wouldn't dare sit around playing on a piano. Both of their skill sets are completely different, nonetheless, they both have everything they need to be great at what they love.

Elizabeth has an amazing pink piano her father had specially made just for her. If she took care of it well, it would last her for many years to come. She felt so special to her father.

One day, the father came home with a beautiful, one-of-a-kind set of pom-poms for Monica because her previous set was stolen. Monica was delighted and she too felt like daddy's special little girl. She very well could not cheer without pom-poms. They were not just a want, but a necessity to do what she loved.

When Elizabeth saw how delighted Monica was and the huge hug and embrace she and her father shared, Elizabeth became jealous and felt it wasn't fair that Monica received a new set of pom-poms. Elizabeth did not consider she already had everything she needed. In the moment, she didn't think about the special relationship she too had with their father and how loved she was by him. She only saw what she didn't receive.

This caused a rift between Elizabeth and her father. For years their relationship was never the same. As long as she "felt" slighted, she held it against her father.

This example seems simple and a little foolish; however, if we're going to be honest, many of us have had a pom-pom mentality for a long time. We've watched God move in the lives of others and we were jealous of how he showed up for them and brought them through. All the while, it "felt" like you were left in a ditch to dig your own way out. You saw God bless people with financial breakthroughs and it "feels" like He left you in your struggle. You saw God bless some of your sisters with a wonderful husband and it "feels" like the only thing that comes your way are the no-good ones. You saw God heal others and you are still experiencing sickness. Just like Elizabeth, as long as you "feel" slighted, you very well may be holding things against God.

Can you identify your pom-poms?

SOMETIMES IT HELPS TO KNOW WHAT YOU ARE NOT

You are not forgettable, you are not replaceable, you are not insignificant. You are invaluable, you have worth, you are needed. For what other reason would Jesus leave

99 for the ONE (1). The world would carry on, but not God. And that's why we have to fix our eyes on Him. If we fix our eyes on people, we will get crushed because we were never meant to carry the weight of comparison, competition and covetousness in the family of God.

When Jesus died on the cross, He had to ask the Father to forgive us. Why? Because we didn't know what we were doing. We didn't know the impact our actions made. Oftentimes, even the most mature, anointed, gifted and well-meaning people would do something thinking it's right and be completely wrong. We all fall short and miss it sometimes. It is so vital for you to keep your eyes on the One who doesn't miss it...EVER. He won't make a mistake and drop you. Blessed is the one who recognizes their need for God. God wants us, He purposefully chose us and yes, He will leave the 99 for YOU.

Leader when you read this, anointed one when you read this, one who is well-versed in Scripture and already know about Jesus leaving the 99—go back and read it again. Don't read it through the lens of one who already knew that or through the lens of one who has been preaching for years, teaching for years, healing the sick, casting out demons and prophesying destinies. I beseech you, read it through the lens of the one who recognizes that yes, I caught myself getting jealous a few times, and sometimes I still feel jealous.

There are many whose title, position and gifts make them feel safe and qualified, but the true knowledge of God's love for them has not sunk deep down into their hearts. As a result, although they are ministering and being used, it is sometimes a struggle to be sustained out of a position of pure love, instead of their ability to perform and operate in gifts and under titles.

If you read this looking through all your goodness, you can miss it. Don't be the Pharisee standing before God feeling accomplished and justified. Be the one who is broken in the presence of God, recognizing your continuous need for a Savior. This requires you to humble yourself and be naked and open before the Lord. Let Him wash you, let Him sanctify you, and let Him justify you.

RECOGNIZE THAT GOD WILL GIVE YOU YOUR HEART'S DESIRE

2 Samuel 12:7-8 NLT

[7] Then Nathan said to David, "You are that man! The LORD, the God of Israel, says: I anointed you king of Israel and saved you from the power of Saul. [8] I gave you your master's house and his wives and the kingdoms of Israel and Judah. And if that had not been enough, I would have given you much, much more.

It is time to truly begin to take a good, in depth look into the mirror. It is time to behold the goodness of the

Lord towards us, His exceedingly great power and riches towards us who believe. Begin to take into account and take an inventory of all the blessings and all the talents he entrusted to us. I'm sure you'll find that you are well endowed.

God is a generous God who supplies all our needs according to His riches in glory in Christ Jesus. He perfects everything that concerns us. Look at how He blessed David and told him if it weren't enough, He would have given him so much more. He wanted and was willing to grant David his heart's desires. We don't have to be covetous of any man or woman or of what they have.

TO KNOW HIS LOVE BY EXPERIENCE

Ephesians 3:17-19 NKJV
[17] that Christ may dwell in your hearts through faith; that you, being rooted and grounded in love, [18] may be able to comprehend with all the saints what is the width and length and depth and height— [19] to know the love of Christ which passes knowledge; that you may be filled with all the fullness of God.

It is imperative that we have our own relationship with God, rooted and grounded in Christ and in His love. For if we are not rooted and grounded, it is likely that we'll be tossed about by many things, including our very own flesh, desires, emotions, the wiles of the enemy and the works of people.

It is easy to be shaken instead of steadfast and immovable, if we're not rooted and grounded. It is easy to stumble and to stress instead of being still if you're not rooted and grounded.

We have to truly grasp and comprehend, with all the saints, all of God's people, the width, length, depth and height of God's love. We have to know it by experience... then we will be made complete.

It is not enough to be able to tell someone else's story, testimony or experience. If you have not had your own experiences and encounters with God, you'll find that even though you genuinely want to be happy for others when you hear how they had multiple encounters and visions of Jesus, you may find yourself wondering, "What about me?"

When you hear testimonies about Jesus Himself giving someone a scroll to eat, showing up in their room, personally handing them a gift that changed their lives and ministry forever, God crowning them as His daughter and putting different types of robes and mantles on them, your human nature may rise up and challenge you. If you have not had your own encounters and experiences, when you hear these things, you may very well question the validity of your own call.

You may wonder if you should have experienced something of this "magnitude" as well. We put labels and levels on everything that ascribe a measure of significance, from low to high, to our lives and our experiences— "Oh, you only had a dream and not an open vision with an encounter with Jesus Himself? Oh, you haven't had an angelic encounter? Oh, you didn't wake up hearing the song of the Lord in the Spirit?" LOL! Can you see how certain behaviors can create schisms and chasms in the body of Christ that leave its members feeling insignificant? God Himself qualifies the called and not the experiences. This is not to say we shouldn't desire wonderful, mind-blowing experiences, because let's face it, we love them and I believe God loves them too. My point is not to disqualify yourself because you didn't have Susie's experience. Let the church say Amen!

Let me tell you, one day as I listened to someone's testimony about how they cried out to God and He spoke to them and told them it wasn't their time to die and that they had work to do, I immediately wanted to say to God, "You didn't do that for me! You spoke to her, in her time of despair, but my experience, in my time of despair, was totally different." Uh, how many of you know that even the thought wasn't a good idea? First, it shows a lack of maturity. Second, it shows a lack of understanding. Thirdly, it shows a lack of knowledge.

I'll let you in on a little secret: You don't know the whole story when people share their experiences with God. You don't know what they've been through to get where they are. It's not that they're trying to be deceitful. However, it is virtually impossible to convey all that was experienced within a simple conversation.

Many of you have tried to tell the "whole" story and when the conversation was over and you parted ways, each one to his own place, you remembered that you forgot something. You say, "Ah man, I wish I would've told them this part, but I completely forgot." Let me tell you, "that part" they forgot, would have changed everything. For the most part, we end up drawing conclusions from fragmented parts of people's memory, which leaves us with a fragmented and faulty response—if we choose to respond.

So, initially, I was about to foolishly charge God with doing something for someone else that He didn't do for me. However, I decided to do the opposite as it also immediately came to me that I'M DIFFERENT. My story is different, my testimony is different, my path and my journey are different. However, just because it's different doesn't mean it's any less God or any less good! God uses us to show His "manifold" wisdom to principalities and powers.

Manifold is the key word. It means in a variety of ways—in different ways, but yet it's still God. Let Him be God and get the glory from your life however He sees fit. We can no longer try to walk and talk like anybody else. We can't try to make their stories our own because we have our own stories to tell. We have our own walk to walk and if we trust God and follow His lead, we will see and learn to appreciate and love the unique plan He graciously prepared just for us. So no longer will we say, "Look what You did for her God; You didn't do that for me." On the contrary, we will begin to thank God for what He did for her and thank God for what He did for us. We will declare...

"It's different, but I know it's God and I know it's good!" God be glorified!

We have to come to the point where we appreciate God's love for us from our own experience with Him and not from the perspective of someone else's experience with Him, which is based on the understanding we have from our outside viewing pleasure.

THE REWARDS OF THE DILIGENT

Let me say this, some people want the rewards of those who diligently seek God, but they have not been consistent or persistent themselves. I'm reminded of the saying, "If you don't work, you don't eat." Some want to eat the fruit of those who labor, but they don't want to work. God loves faithfulness. Some have sown and are reaping bountifully; they have poured out their lives and God is showing up mightily on their behalf. If "YOU" seek, will you not find?

Don't get thrown off course; He wants you to know His love by experience. Since we are looking in the mirror, ask yourself how deep your intimacy is with God. Evaluate your ways and see if you are seeking Him with all of your heart, because He promises that if we seek, we will find. Check your level of importunity. Check to see if your knocking is persistent and consistent, because He will open the door for you. Above all things, do you desire to walk in close fellowship with Him? It's not just available for a select few—a right relationship with God is available to all of us.

FINDING YOUR REHOBOTH

Gen 26:22 NLT
Abandoning that one, Isaac moved on and dug another well. This time there was no dispute over it, so Isaac named the place Rehoboth (which means "open space"),

for he said, "At last the LORD has created enough space for us to prosper in this land."

It's time to abandon, as Isaac had done, those places in our hearts that caused disputes with our brothers and sisters in Christ. We can no longer attempt to lay claim to the wells others have dug. We can see in chapter 26 of Genesis how when Isaac's servants discovered wells of fresh water, two times they were disputed over. He had to name those places "argument" and "hostility," move forward and leave them behind.

How many arguments and how much hostility has been created in the body of Christ because God has been blessing His servants? We see people becoming wealthy and just like the Philistines, we've become jealous and filled their wells with dirt—slander, accusation, back-biting, cruelty, hatred, dishonor, disrespect, etc. We've abandoned many, deserted many, ostracized many, and kicked out many telling them to go somewhere else because you didn't like how powerful they have become.

Guess what, God was still with Isaac, blessing him and allowing him to discover new wells. God is faithful and He keeps His promises. He is no respecter of persons. He will do the same for you if you are faithful to Him and keep His requirements, commands, decrees and instructions as Abraham had done (Genesis 26:5 NLT).

God is delighted to bless you! "Let the LORD be magnified, Who has pleasure in the prosperity of His servant." Psalm 35:27b NKJV

Isaac "moved on and dug another well." It's time to move on from the place of jealousy and dig your well. There is fresh water waiting to be discovered by you—rivers of living water that are in you, waiting to be discovered and embraced by you!

There is a Rehoboth—an open space that God has created for you to prosper in and I tell you there won't be any disputes over it! When you operate in the space God has given you, people will be able to see plainly that He is with you. Find your Rehoboth, find your place, your lane, your well from which you can continuously draw and be renewed in your mind, restored in your soul, refreshed in your spirit and begin to bring glory to the Lord, your God.

Declare it with me: "The disputes, arguments and hostility are OVER!"

7

THE FIGHT AGAINST JEALOUSY

Declaration: I will put on the full armor of God!

Psalm 18:37 NKJV
I have pursued my enemies and overtaken them;
Neither did I turn back again till they were destroyed.

THIS IS IT!

Listen! When you stand in the face of the enemy who comes in the form of jealousy, or any form for that matter, don't get discouraged and frustrated. Discouragement and frustration are tools of the enemy to distract you from the jealousy that is currently standing before you trying to oppose you and destroy you.

Remember, Satan waits for a more opportune time to come against you. He is an opportunist. So, when something happens and jealousy rises and rears its ugly head, don't get discouraged that it's there.

I know—I know, you don't want to feel that jealousy. When you prayed for God to help you, what you wanted was for Him to just take it away so you wouldn't have to deal with it anymore. You don't want to stand and fight against this spirit.

Let me encourage you. Every time jealousy gets bold enough to confront you, it is YOUR OPPORTUNE time to turn the table on the enemy. It is your chance to humble yourself before God, resist the devil and make him flee. It is your chance to choose God and not what the enemy is serving. It is your chance to use the weapons of God that are not carnal, but mighty through God to the pulling down of strongholds. It is your chance to declare a blessing over your life and not a curse. It is your chance to be victorious and not defeated.

It feels difficult in the moment. You are frustrated that you even have to deal with it, you hate it and it doesn't feel good at all, but every time you go to battle against jealousy and you overcome, you are a step closer to winning the war!

Please remember, we are not fighting against flesh and blood, but against principalities, powers, the rulers of the darkness of this age, and spiritual wickedness in high places.

With each battle you are getting stronger! Don't let the enemy deceive you. You may feel weak because jealousy keeps popping up. Your maturity, naturally and in Christ is questioned, your integrity is questioned, your character is questioned, your sincerity is questioned, your love for God and people is questioned, your loyalty and faithfulness are questioned—all to the point where you wonder, "God, am I even a good person?" You feel like a hot mess.

Let me encourage you: Be strong in the Lord and in the power of His might! It's not by your power nor by your might, it's by His Spirit! God has given you the grace to win every battle and win the war. How? It has already been won in Christ Jesus. He already disarmed the enemy and made a public spectacle of him.

Isaiah 41:13 (NIV)
For I am the LORD your God
    who takes hold of your right hand
and says to you, Do not fear;
    I will help you.

Joshua 1:9 (NIV)

Have I not commanded you? Be strong and coura-geous. Do not be afraid; do not be discouraged, for the LORD your God will be with you wherever you go."

Isaiah 41:10 (NLT)

Don't be afraid, for I am with you.

Don't be discouraged, for I am your God.

I will strengthen you and help you.

I will hold you up with my victorious right hand.

Every time we stand in the midst of a battle, you can either say, "God, why me?" or you can say, "God, thank You for fighting against those who fight against me. The battle has already been won and my victory is sure!"

Let me assure you, if you are reading this book, YOU WILL NOT BE DEFEATED! The very fact that this book is in your hands says you want to win. God has already or-dained your victory and you will see it! You will see your enemy defeated before your very eyes. You will not be the one who goes down! Why?

It was for this reason the Son of God was made manifest, to destroy the works of the devil!

Come on...shout HALLELUJAH to the Lamb of God, who was slain before the foundation of the world!

Yes! We overcome by the blood of the Lamb and the word of our testimony!

Let the works of the Lord be made manifest in your life!

Choose this day whom you will serve! You don't serve jealousy; you serve the one and only, true and living God. The enemy, even jealousy, is under your feet!

Joshua 10:24-25 NLT

[24] When they brought them out, Joshua told the commanders of his army, "Come and put your feet on the kings' necks." And they did as they were told.

[25] "Don't ever be afraid or discouraged," Joshua told his men. "Be strong and courageous, for the LORD is going to do this to all of your enemies."

This day, the Lord gives jealousy unto you—will you step on its neck?

So how do you fight? We're going to get our marching orders, strategy and instruction from the tried and true Word of God.

Ephesians 6:13-18 (NKJV)

¹³ Therefore take up the whole armor of God, that you may be able to withstand in the evil day, and having done all, to stand.

¹⁴ Stand therefore, having girded your waist with truth, having put on the breastplate of righteousness, ¹⁵ and having shod your feet with the preparation of the gospel of peace; ¹⁶ above all, taking the shield of faith with which you will be able to quench all the fiery darts of the wicked one. ¹⁷ And take the helmet of salvation, and the sword of the Spirit, which is the word of God; ¹⁸ praying always with all prayer and supplication in the Spirit, being watchful to this end with all perseverance and supplication for all the saints—

Let's break this down verse by verse from 13-18:

1. TAKE YOUR STANCE!

¹³ Therefore take up the whole armor of God that you may be able to withstand in the evil day, and having done all, to stand. ¹⁴Stand therefore,...

Determine in your heart and mind that you will stand. We know that the Lord will not suffer the righteous to be moved.

Make up in your mind that you will be steadfast and unmovable!

Make up in your mind that you are going to fight the good fight of faith.

Make up in your mind that NO WEAPON FORMED AGAINST YOU SHALL PROSPER!

Know that this too shall pass.

Let's look at 2 Corinthians 4:17 (NKJV)

For our light affliction, which is but for a moment, worketh for us a far more exceeding and eternal weight of glory;

2 Corinthians 4:16-18 (MSG)
So we're not giving up. How could we! Even though on the outside it often looks like things are falling apart on us, on the inside, where God is making new life, not a day goes by without his unfolding grace. These hard times are small potatoes compared to the coming good times, the lavish celebration prepared for us. There's far more here than meets the eye. The things we see now are here today, gone tomorrow. But the things we can't see now will last forever.

Kick that defeated attitude to the curb, because it will not allow you to stand. It will get in the way of victory every time. Victory and a defeated mindset are enemies.

2. YOUR BELT HOLDS EVERYTHING TOGETHER!

¹⁴ Stand therefore, having girded your waist with truth,

There is nothing like the truth. The truth holds everything together, even when we want to fall apart. It is the truth that sets us free. His Word is truth. His Word is sharper than any double-edged sword. His Word is a discerner of the thoughts and intents of the heart (Hebrews 4:12).

When we are overcoming this spirit of jealousy we need the thoughts and intents of the heart discerned, both ours and others.

We can't afford to lack the knowledge of the truth. We can't afford to lean unto our own understanding. It is the Word of the Lord and His Word alone that will stand. So, if His Word alone will stand, we can't afford to stand on anything else, if we truly want to be victorious.

We are not entertaining the logic and reasoning of men, at this point. Logic and reason may fail, but the Word of the Lord is sure.

I beseech you, in all your getting, get understanding. This is key when dealing with a spirit of jealousy. It is the knowledge and understanding of the truth that will combat and pull down all of the lies and deception.

3. COVER YOUR BREASTS!

[14]...having put on the breastplate of righteousness,

There is power in righteousness! Period. We know from 2 Corinthians 6:7 righteousness is a weapon, it is a part of our armor. Remember, we are human, but we don't wage war as humans do. Hallelujah! Righteousness is mighty in God to the pulling down of strongholds.

Let the righteousness of Christ go before you.

Because He made Him who knew no sin, to be sin for us, that we might become the righteousness of God in Him (2 Corinthians 5:21 NJKV).

Remember, in order for us to be able to stand firm against all strategies of the devil, we have to put on ALL of God's armor, and this includes righteousness.

The good news is that God is willing to cleanse us of all unrighteousness.

1 John 1:9 NKJV

If we confess our sins, He is faithful and just to forgive us our sins and to cleanse us from all unrighteousness.

We may have messed up before, given power to jealousy and walked in the wrong spirit, but we can come boldly before God's throne of grace. There is no condemnation for those who are in Christ Jesus.

So, let us get cleansed—we have work to do—together!

4. PUT ON THE RIGHT SHOES!

[15] and having shod your feet with the preparation of the gospel of peace

Consider how you walk in sandals, high heels and sneakers. In sneakers your walk is more secure, it is stronger, your stride is different and you're able to cover more ground in a shorter time frame. The sneakers give you the support you need as you move forward so you're not distracted by the instability or fragility (the quality of being easily broken or damaged) of a sandal or high heel shoe.

Your feet are divinely designed for you to stand. The covering of your feet is critical and can make all the difference in your flight and your fight. There's a time when it's great to walk in your heels and you move with confidence and a little more pep in your step, there's a time for the sandal where you can relax in your leisure and then there's the time for your sneakers. Know your times! This is a spiritual battle and you need to be stable, strong, sturdy and steadfast.

Your mind can't be weak and fragile; you need to be focused and have your mind stayed on Christ. You can't be easily broken in your mind, your heart or your spirit man. This battle requires you to be strong in the Lord and in the power of His might. This battle requires you to be sober and vigilant. You can't be ignorant of the wiles of the enemy. You have to be discerning and you have to be honest. Denial and pretenses are open doors that will keep you bound.

You must be willing to be naked before the Lord so that He can wash you; for, if the Lord washes you, you will be made clean. Don't ignore or tolerate the signs or the manifestations, deal with it once and for all. There are some spirits we don't need to keep giving carte blanche to rear its ugly head. It is to these spirits we need to declare, "you can't go where I'm going," and stop saying this to our brothers and sisters in Christ. We are one family, one body jointly fit together and if we can't go with each other, we are divided, fragmented and DISMEMBERED. Remember our fight is not against flesh and blood. **TELL THOSE DEMONS THEY CAN'T GO!**

We have to put on our shoes and begin to walk circumspectly—watchful, with caution and with vigilance.

Ephesians 5:15-17 NKJV

[15] See then that you walk circumspectly, not as fools but as wise, [16] redeeming the time, because the days are evil.

[17] Therefore do not be unwise, but understand what the will of the Lord is.

5. POWER SHIELD OF FAITH!

[16] above all, taking the shield of faith with which you will be able to quench all the fiery darts of the wicked one.

This really excites me! Our faith is literally a shield that puts out every fiery dart of the wicked one. Our faith can literally subvert every attack of our enemy.

Let us see the spirit of jealousy completely overthrown. Our faith and our love which is in Christ Jesus will not fail us.

Let's look at the power of faith:

Hebrews 11:33-34 NLT

[33] By faith these people overthrew kingdoms, ruled with justice, and received what God had promised them. They shut the mouths of lions, [34] quenched the flames of

fire, and escaped death by the edge of the sword. Their weakness was turned to strength. They became strong in battle and put whole armies to flight.

Are you ready to put jealousy to flight? God has made us strong for the battle through our faith.

6. COVER YOUR HEADS!

[17] And take the helmet of salvation,

We really must have our minds renewed. We must allow God to transform us into a new person by changing the way we think. It is then we will be able to prove what is that good, acceptable and perfect will of God (Romans 12:2).

The Lord is our salvation, He alone is our deliverer.

2 Samuel 22:3-4 NKJV
[3] The God of my strength, in whom I will trust;
My shield and the horn of my salvation,
My stronghold and my refuge;
My Savior, You save me from violence.
[4] I will call upon the LORD, who is worthy to be praised;
So shall I be saved from my enemies.

7. PUT AWAY THAT KNIFE!

[17]...and the sword of the Spirit, which is the word of God;

We know we are not wrestling against flesh and blood. You have a sword that is alive, powerful and approved by God. Stop wielding the weapons of this world. You shouldn't have to worry about whether or not someone's going to stab you in the back.

The weapons of our warfare are not carnal. They are mighty through God to the pulling down of strongholds. In this fight, we are using God's weapons to pull down the stronghold of jealousy. Carnal weapons will only work against us.

Don't be lured by the ease and the availability of a spiritual knife the enemy would put in your hands—don't be deceived by the way it shines or its sharpness. You have something far greater and it will never work against you or your brothers and sisters in Christ. It will accomplish what is best for all. It will not fail.

8. SIMPLY PRAY!

[18] praying always with all prayer and supplication in the Spirit, being watchful to this end with all perseverance and supplication for all the saints—

There is so much power in praying in the Spirit. You may not know how to pray as you ought to concerning the situation. You may have some blind spots because you are caught up in your feelings. There may be mental and emotional strongholds of which you are not yet aware. You also may be ignorant of how the enemy is employing strategies—subtle and cunning wiles against the relationship. Also keep in mind, you have no idea what the other person is going through, have walked through and have had to endure. Your prayers are needed to cover all parties involved. When praying in the Spirit, you can be sure that your prayers won't be selfish, going forth with impure motives or in vain. These prayers won't fall to the ground or miss the mark. Pray earnestly in the Spirit.

Pray and ask for prayer!

Don't be ashamed or embarrassed to ask for prayer.

James 5:16 NLT
Confess your sins to each other and pray for each other so that you may be healed. The earnest prayer of a righteous person has great power and produces wonderful results.

It's time to get healed and delivered. We've read how critical it is to overcome this spirit of jealousy so that the body of Christ can be united and undivided. You are required to do your part and by any means necessary, whatever it takes, get your deliverance!

9. OVERCOMING WITH LOVE

We have to come to the understanding, beyond a shadow of doubt, that without love we have truly missed it. Why are we still trying to press forward to do great exploits, to prophesy, to heal the sick, to work miracles and not have love as our motivation? Many are pressing forward toward the work of the ministry, but we do not want to love the people. This is far from the heart of God. We have come to this place where we want many to follow us, but we do not want to care for them. When the multitudes followed Jesus into the wilderness, He did not just preach to them and go on about His business. He was concerned for them, He had love and compassion for them, such that He refused to send them away hungry—He knew they wouldn't make it; He knew they would faint and He cared. It was out of His love for the people that brought about the second miracle of the multiplication of food. He didn't just feed them spiritually; He took care of their natural need. What good would it have been to pour into them spiritually, to heal them and have them faint from natural hunger on their way back?

Matthew 15:32 NLT
Then Jesus called his disciples and told them, "I feel sorry for these people. They have been here with me for

three days, and they have nothing left to eat. I don't want to send them away hungry, or they will faint along the way."

1 Corinthians 13:1-7 NLT

If I could speak all the languages of earth and of angels, but didn't love others, I would only be a noisy gong or a clanging cymbal. 2 If I had the gift of prophecy, and if I understood all of God's secret plans and possessed all knowledge, and if I had such faith that I could move mountains, but didn't love others, I would be nothing. 3 If I gave everything I have to the poor and even sacrificed my body, I could boast about it; but if I didn't love others, I would have gained nothing.

4 Love is patient and kind. Love is not jealous or boastful or proud 5 or rude. It does not demand its own way. It is not irritable, and it keeps no record of being wronged. 6 It does not rejoice about injustice but rejoices whenever the truth wins out. 7 Love never gives up, never loses faith, is always hopeful, and endures through every circumstance.

Considering our topic at hand, overcoming jealousy, it's going to take a total shift in the way we've done things. It's going to take letting patience have her perfect work in us, it's going to take us being kind to one another. It's going to take us no longer having the need to be puffed up and praised, no longer being rude and making excuses for it, no more demanding our own way, and no more being easily irritated over the smallest things. Yes, it's going to take letting go of how he wronged you and how she did you wrong. It's no longer rejoicing when things go wrong for people (yes, I know you didn't rejoice outwardly and no one else knew). It's going to take rejoicing over the truth. It's going to take not giving up and throwing in the towel on people. It's going to take believing in others and in what God is doing through them. It's going to take being hopeful for others and enduring through every circumstance with the right heart and the right spirit.

10. GRACE

The bonus weapon of grace!

James 4:6 NLT
And he gives grace generously. As the Scriptures say,
"God opposes the proud
but gives grace to the humble."

Let us keep in mind that the grace of God is sufficient and in our weakness God's power is perfected.

Humbling ourselves before God should be a very comfortable place for us.

There is actually a throne of grace! God wants us to come boldly before Him in humility, ready to help us in our time of need. There is grace to help. Hallelujah!

11. FORGIVENESS

We can't leave this fight without the subject of forgiveness. How can we win with unforgiveness in our hearts?

Some of you have either been hurt by people, have hurt other people or both because of this spirit. This is not the time to rehash and be angry, it's not the time to point fingers or push blame, it's not the time to be a victim, though we recognize that many have been caught in the crossfire.

Now is the time to be true sons and daughters of the Most High God and take our rightful places as PEACEMAKERS who are ready and willing to forgive and walk in love, by the power of the Holy Spirit. You don't have to do it in your own strength, but you do have to be willing. Now is the time for us to unite and walk in unity in the bond of peace. We need to love each other as God, who is our everlasting Father, desires for us to love each other. This is what any father wants for his children. Loving each other can no longer be foreign or just in your small circle and no more. Now is the time to expand our borders...the borders of our hearts. Now is the time to extend our reach. Those records of wrongdoing that we've kept in our heart and mind—let's destroy them. Those times we've rejoiced at injustice—let's repent. It's time to walk in love, it's time to unite and it's time to rebuild.

To sum it all up, what does it actually take to overcome this spirit of jealousy?

1. You will first have to take a stance—no hesitation, no reservation, no wavering, no denial, and no tolerance.
2. TRUTH—be determined that you will walk in truth.
3. Righteousness—this is the Kingdom. Period.
4. Peace—God gave us His peace. It will cover and guard our hearts and minds in Christ Jesus.
5. Faith—this is your shield, your protection and it will overcome jealousy.
6. Salvation—have your mind set on the truth that God will deliver you.
7. The Word of God—this will help you stand through the battle and ensure your victory.
8. Prayer—pray without ceasing for all of God's people everywhere.
9. Love—how can we continue to say we love God and not keep His command to love one another? This is not an option or an elective activity, it is a command.
10. Grace—His grace is sufficient!
11. Forgiveness—People have and will trespass against you. Determine in your heart to walk in forgiveness. God will forgive you as you forgive those who trespass against you. (Matthew 6:12, Luke 17:4)

HAVE I OVERCOME?

How do I know if I still have jealousy in my heart? I've prayed, cast it out and asked God to remove it. First, you can ask God if it's still there. Second, you can look at your fruit—how you respond to things. For instance, if someone is receiving praise and you get those twinges in your heart (it may feel like a change in the regular rhythm of your heart beat), you might need to check the source. If you hear about or read about something great happening in another person's life and your heart beat dips, slows down or accelerates and you notice it changed (and it wasn't a good change), it may be something there you need to pray into.

HEART CHECK!

Whether jealousy is prompted by seeing someone successful, seeing someone receive praise, seeing someone receive something you would like to have, or seeing someone blessed, you can try asking yourself this: Do I have everything I need? Am I exactly where God wants me to be? Do I have everything God wants me to have? If the answer is no, talk to God about it. You already know He wants to bless you. You already know He wants you to prosper, you already know He won't withhold any good thing from those who love him and walk in righteousness, you already know He's planned wonderful things for you, you already know He loves you, you already know He'll make all grace abound toward you so that you will have all sufficiency for every good work, you already know He wants you to be fruitful. What He doesn't want is for you to be covetous. What He doesn't want is for you to ask amiss—with the wrong heart or wrong motive. What He doesn't want is for you to doubt (to feel uncertain about whether or not He's going to do it for you) when you come to Him.

So...talk to Him. Each day surrender your will to His will. Ask Him to search your heart and if there's anything not like Him that needs to be removed. Ask Him to reveal and to remove any hardness in your heart.

If you are not yet at a place where you can hear Him clearly, simply pray—and be sure to make it a priority to learn to hear His voice. Take joy in knowing that He hears YOU clearly, even those things you can't find the words to express.

Sometimes when we see someone blessed, their blessing might prompt in us a desire to acquire something we do not have. Something might be said in prayer or in a regular conversation that will awaken something in us that says, "Wait a minute, that's a promise from God to all of His children and I don't see it in my life."

Go to God and ask Him if now is a good time for you to have it, ask if there are any hindrances, ask if repentance is needed for anything you're doing or have done that would keep you from receiving it. If all is in right standing, ask Him to release it to you.

Let me say this, just because you ask God to bless you with something that you see someone else with or receive, doesn't necessarily mean your prompting is coming from jealousy, but always be honest with yourself and check your heart. Remember, He said you have not because you ask not and even when you ask, you ask amiss. It's okay if you recognize the source is jealousy, don't condemn yourself, beat yourself up, feel guilty or ashamed, just get free!

James 3:13-15 NLT

[13] If you are wise and understand God's ways, prove it by living an honorable life, doing good works with the humility that comes from wisdom. [14] But if you are bitterly jealous and there is selfish ambition in your heart, don't cover up the truth with boasting and lying. [15] For jealousy and selfishness are not God's kind of wisdom. Such things are earthly, unspiritual, and demonic.

The fight against jealousy will really take a deep, sincere and thorough examination of your heart. This fight is not surface level—surface level will keep all kinds of evil intentions of the heart hidden. We have to become like David and pursue God's own heart. David was so serious that He prayed in Psalm 19:12-14 NLT:

[12] How can I know all the sins lurking in my heart?

Cleanse me from these hidden faults.
¹³ Keep your servant from deliberate sins!
    Don't let them control me.
Then I will be free of guilt
    and innocent of great sin.
¹⁴ May the words of my mouth
    and the meditation of my heart
be pleasing to you,
    O LORD, my rock and my redeemer.

David wasn't playing games. He understood that the condition of his heart, if not cleansed, could cause him to be in sin. He wanted to be free of both guilt and sin. He wanted what he spoke from his mouth and what he thought and felt in his heart to be pleasing to God. We can't be satisfied with saying and doing the right things, yet our hearts are far from God and from people.

We can't be afraid to go deep. Many of us want to go deeper into the things of God, but we don't want to check our hearts. It is truly time to say:

Psalm 139:23-24 NKJV
²³ Search me, O God, and know my heart;
Try me, and know my anxieties;
²⁴ And see if there is any wicked way in me,
And lead me in the way everlasting.

Checking our hearts may be unnerving and unsettling. For some, checking our hearts and finding out what's rooted in it can be quite daunting and overwhelming, but it is very necessary.

Before you go out and conquer the world, be courageous enough to confront what's in you.

We all know that our heart is a vital organ in our physical body. From the Word, we also know that the spiritual condition of our heart also directly affects our natural bodies. The bible says that jealousy is like cancer in the bones. CANCER!!!

Proverbs 14:30 NLT
A peaceful heart leads to a healthy body;
  jealousy is like cancer in the bones.

I would beseech you to make every effort to cultivate and maintain a peaceful heart—a heart that is undefiled and has no wicked way in it. Make it your prayer that the peace of God would truly rule and reign in your heart.

Wow—not only does jealousy affect your physical individual body, but it affects the "body" of Christ.

Colossians 3:14-15 NLT

¹⁴ Above all, clothe yourselves with love, which binds us all together in perfect harmony. ¹⁵ And let the peace that comes from Christ rule in your hearts. For as members of one body you are called to live in peace. And always be thankful.

In this fight against jealousy, our primary and most effective weapon is LOVE. The Bible explicitly tells us in 1 Corinthians 13:4 that LOVE IS NOT JEALOUS. You can NOT walk in love and have jealousy rule in your heart at the same time. If you think you have been walking in love and have not dealt with the jealousy in your heart, it's time to deal with it. I don't care if it only pops up once a year, I want you to make sure there are no roots, houses or open doors. Let your heart be purified.

Ask God, Himself, to search you. We can be quick to say, "this is not my problem." The real problem is, we don't know what is hidden unless God reveals it. Remember, humble yourself and take the posture of David. We need every hidden fault to be revealed. Also, as you walk in love, just as Jesus told Peter, after you've been strengthened, strengthen your brothers and sisters. Please don't sit back and say, "I'm ok, I'm straight," when your brothers and sisters are bound and in battle. Don't leave them on the battlefield alone. This is not the way of the Lord.

Remember, when the tribes of Reuben, Gad and Manasseh received their lot, they weren't able to sit back and chill—they had to continue to fight until everyone received their land. We can't be satisfied with just our deliverance, we want everyone to be delivered. We are one body; when one suffers, we all suffer.

I wasn't going to include the account regarding this, but I think it's a powerful call to the soldiers in the army of God, men and women, to rise up and fight for each other. We can't take the stance of Cain who was jealous, took the life of his brother and asked God if he was his brother's keeper. Warriors rise up! This is all of our fight!

Joshua 1:12-15 NLT

[12] Then Joshua called together the tribes of Reuben, Gad, and the half-tribe of Manasseh. He told them, [13] "Remember what Moses, the servant of the LORD, commanded you: 'The LORD your God is giving you a place of rest. He has given you this land.' [14] Your wives, children, and livestock may remain here in the land Moses assigned to you on the east side of the Jordan River. But your strong warriors, fully armed, must lead the other tribes across the Jordan to help them conquer their territory. Stay with them [15] until the LORD gives them rest, as he has given you rest, and until they, too, possess the land the LORD your God is giving them. Only then may you return and settle here on the east side of the Jordan River in the land that Moses, the servant of the LORD, assigned to you."

It is bigger than you, yet it includes you! Check your heart!

8

FIX YOUR EYES ON JESUS

Declaration: From no other place does my help come! It is in Him I live, breathe and have my being!

WHAT I SEE IS UP TO ME!

In this hour, it is of critical necessity to keep our eyes fixed on Jesus. There is a work that needs to be done in the earth that only the children of God can accomplish. Each and every one of us is needed to fulfill our part as a member of the body of Christ.

We can't lose sight of the truth that there is one body with many members. We are a body jointly fit together to do the will of the Father.

I was greatly encouraged when I read in His Word that He was pleased with where and how He placed each and every one of us in the body of Christ. Let's go ahead and make this very personal...God was and is very pleased with where He put you in the body of Christ. It is your privilege and honor to fulfill the call of God on your life and to walk in the works He prepared just for you.

Let us not fall for the trap of the enemy that would have us looking to the right and to the left and getting discouraged because of what our brothers and sisters are doing.

I've recognized a trigger point of jealousy upon which I've pondered and prayed.

You see, oftentimes, we would recognize a need for something or we will have a desire for something that we can't articulate or give language to, yet our souls cry out for it. We are not always able to put our finger on the very thing we have a deep yearning for (sometimes we are). We'll first recognize what we've been crying out for in someone else. We'll see the very thing we want and need present in someone else's life. At the lowest level, for instance, we'll see someone with the house we want or the marriage we want. When it goes a little deeper, we'll see someone with the intimate relationship with God that we yearn for or operating in the gifts of the Spirit the way we hope to, being used by God in a powerful way that we want to, or we'll see people experiencing wild success, uncommon victories, and prospering greatly. Then when our soul is awakened due to the recognition of what it's been crying out for, we are then placed at a crossroad.

Down one path, we can go before the Lord in prayer, thanking Him for allowing us to put words to or witness the longing in our hearts. We are then able to ask in prayer, not amiss, for the petitions of our heart.

Down the other path is what the enemy would place before us when we recognize what we desire present in or with someone else. The enemy would present jealousy to you. He would cause you to question God's love for you, His plans for you and His call on your life. The enemy would pervert the experience, causing you to feel slighted, abandoned, forgotten, less than, unworthy, and under-valued instead of God's divine love that opened your eyes and allowed you to see exactly what you need and want and what He is "willing" to give you.

God told us in His Word, "I don't give as the world gives." John 14:27

Look at how salvation was offered to the Gentiles: [11] Did God's people stumble and fall beyond recovery? Of course not! They were disobedient, so God made salvation available to the Gentiles. But He wanted his own people to become jealous and claim it for themselves. Romans 11:11 NLT

He did it to draw the Jews to Him, not to separate them from Him. However, what the world gives to you would draw you from God.

So, when you see your brother or sister walking in the blessings you desire, know that it is the love of God, for both them and you. You are not left out, God has opened your eyes to draw you to Himself and it's up to you to guard your heart with all diligence and make sure it is open to the love of the Father and not the wiles of the enemy.

You get to decide if you're going to choose jealousy or thankfulness and gratitude.

YOU ARE THE LOVED ONE, SO WHY BE JEALOUS?

Do you remember the unfortunate circumstances and the drama that took place between Rachel and Leah? It is so obvious why Leah was jealous of Rachel, yet the bible expressly mentions that Rachel was jealous of Leah.

Rachel and Leah shared the same husband; however, Rachel was the one whom Jacob loved—Jacob was smitten with Rachel. Leah on the other hand, uh...she just didn't have any "sparkle."

The Bible says that when God saw that Leah was unloved, he enabled her to have children, but Rachel could not conceive (Genesis 29:31 NLT). Leah kept pushing out children back to back and giving Jacob son after son. After Leah's fourth son was born, Rachel realized something wasn't quite right and she became jealous of her sister. Let's look at the Scripture, so that I can make my point:

Genesis 30:1-3 NLT
When Rachel saw that she wasn't having any children for Jacob, she became jealous of her sister. She pleaded with Jacob, "Give me children, or I'll die!"

[2] Then Jacob became furious with Rachel. "Am I God?" he asked. "He's the one who has kept you from having children!"

[3] Then Rachel told him, "Take my maid, Bilhah, and sleep with her. She will bear children for me, and through her I can have a family, too."

Be careful that in your jealousy, you don't reproduce out of another spirit.

Be careful that in your jealousy, you don't try to reproduce out of another woman's womb and take it as your own.

Yes, you might see others being extremely fruitful and every time you turn around they are giving birth to something new. It seems like everything their hands touch prospers. Every time you look there is a new business, a new ministry, another book, another conference, another engagement, or another connection.

Like Rachel, you begin to cry out, "I know that I am loved by God, but why am I not fruitful?" You even begin to entertain the thoughts that you must've done something wrong.

Can I tell you, YOU didn't do anything wrong! Rachel didn't do anything wrong. God is sovereign and in His sovereignty, He opened up Leah's womb and made her fruitful. In His sovereignty, He was merciful and gracious toward Leah and it did not mean that He loved Rachel any less, for there came a time when Rachel bore a son from her own womb.

Be careful that in the waiting you don't falsely place blame on people for what you deem as a lack of fruitfulness on your end. Be careful that you don't wrongly accuse people because you don't see what God is doing in your own life. The bible says that Rachel pleaded with Jacob, "Give me children, or I'll die!" Jacob then became furious and had to put her in her place: "Am I God?" he asked. "He's the one who has kept you from having children!" (Genesis 30:2)

Don't you know, in its time, God will cause you to come forth and give birth to something greater than you ever imagined? Rachel gave birth to Joseph, who was used mightily to save the nation of Israel. What God has for you is great too!

Don't look at the fruitfulness of the "Leahs" and discount the magnitude of God's love for you and His plans for your life—what you carry is significant!

Galatians 6:4-5 NLT

[4] Pay careful attention to your own work, for then you will get the satisfaction of a job well done, and you won't need to compare yourself to anyone else. [5] For we are each responsible for our own conduct.

Don't be moved when you see others prospering. It is all to the glory of the Lord, our God. You are responsible for the way you conduct yourself. You are responsible for your actions and the way you respond when you see the work of others. Don't go trying to force things to happen outside of God's will or His timing.

Know that your womb is fruitful and no two people can ever give birth to the exact same thing, so expect what you bring forth to be different, to be unique, to be blessed and to be significant.

AS UNTO THE LORD

Let everything you say or do be to the glory of God. Make sure your motives are pure. Don't be afraid to check your heart. Sometimes we say or do things and we know good and well it didn't come from a pure place—it sounded good and it looked good and the people high-fived, applauded and said Amen, but YOU know, it was birthed out of jealousy, YOU know the spirit behind it wasn't the Holy Spirit. It's time to repent and ask God to see if there is any wicked way in us, if perhaps you can't pinpoint exactly what the root cause is.

Have no expectations of man and do not love their praise more than the praise of God. Don't expect their praise, don't expect their recognition, don't expect their agreement, don't expect their confirmation, don't expect their affirmation, and don't expect their consideration of you. When I say don't expect, I also mean not to depend on these things. I'm sure you have found out by now that sometimes our "expectations" can get us into trouble. Perhaps when you "expected" a praise and didn't get one, or perhaps when you expected agreement or consideration and it didn't come, how did you handle it?

Your help comes from God, your promotion comes from God, your affirmation comes from God. He will send confirmation—let God Himself honor you, let Him open doors and make ways, let Him present opportunities, let Him make the connections with people.

You don't have to do anything extra or be anything extra – By the grace of God, You are who and what you are. 1 Corinthians 15:10

When you have given God His proper place in your life, you no longer (mis)place people in your life or assign false roles, false expectations, and false responsibilities on people who God didn't send to do what you "think" they should do. For the most part, people only know you to the extent that you are able to properly reveal yourself. There is a part of you that natural ears or natural eyes can't perceive, except it be revealed by God.

You can only be completely open and naked before God. There's no where you can retreat and hide from Him.

IT'S GOING TO REQUIRE THE HELP OF JESUS

Look at what Jesus said to His disciples, "Do not let your hearts be troubled. You believe in God; believe also in me." John 14:1 NIV.

In overcoming, we can give ourselves a million pep talks, we can try to avoid the trap of jealousy, we can really want to change, but sometimes that change doesn't come until we put our trust in God. If we continue to tell ourselves to get it together and girl don't fall for it, we can have this same argument over and over and over again. We might be able to shake "the feeling" at that moment, but it will come back again with the same person or another person, if it is not properly dealt with. We have to start standing on the truth of who God is and who He is for us.

When something happens that arouses jealousy, we have to remember who God is. When someone is being promoted, given honor, special treatment, or receiving praise, applause and accolades, don't succumb to those feelings that start to drown you out with bitter envy—fix your eyes on the Lord and declare who He is:

"Lord You are righteous; You are a just God. You are a good God and a wonderful Father to me. God, I know You won't withhold any good thing from me. Father I magnify You over this jealousy, because I know You delight in my prosperity. I know I am accepted by You and unconditionally loved by You. God, I know You will gladly make my efforts successful as well. God, I know it is Your will for me to be fruitful in every good work and you prepared work just for me. You have a plan for my life and it isn't a replication of anyone else's. Father Your timing for everything in my life to come to pass is perfect. I will wait on You Lord, I will trust You. Help me to be more patient and to walk in Your perfect peace as I patiently wait for everything to unfold in its time. Father may my joy be full in You, not in people or things. Father if I'm lacking in the knowledge of Your will, fill me and give me wisdom and spiritual understanding that I may walk worthy of You and be fully pleasing to You. In Jesus Name, Amen!"

DON'T MISS HIM!

Please don't be so busy with your eyes on others that when Jesus shows up, He can walk right past you and you know it not. He comes knocking and you do not hear. He comes with opportunity, but you don't perceive it because your heart has become so hardened from focusing on the goings-on in the lives of others, that you don't recognize what God is trying to accomplish in your own.

You are unable to appreciate what God is doing in your life because your expectations are built up based on what you think you see God doing for someone else. You're comparing and despising, comparing and discounting, comparing and discrediting, so every time you look at what's in your hand, it's deemed inferior and not good enough. In this state, you may never be satisfied because your appetite is that of the flesh and of the flesh you reap death.

Change your focus and sow into the Spirit and follow after the Spirit so that you can begin to reap Spiritual things that bring life and life more abundantly. Therein lies your true peace and true joy. May your harvest be plentiful.

"YOU, FOLLOW ME."

Jesus said to him, "If I will that he remain till I come, what is that to you? You follow Me." John 21:22 NKJV

Jesus has called each and every one of us to follow Him. While you are walking with Him, don't get distracted and look back. In looking back, you may not be able to handle what you see. Looking back may cause you to start asking unnecessary questions that have nothing to do with you. Looking back can take you off course because you become curious about what God is doing in someone else's life and you begin to wonder what they had to go through, if they had to suffer, or if they paid the price. Peter looked back and saw the one whom Jesus loved following also. Have you ever looked around and thought, "What is she doing here?" Have you ever wanted it to be, "just you?"

There may be times where we would really need to consider the question Jesus posed to Peter in order to keep things in perspective, **"What is it to you?"** You would often find that you don't have an answer. So, stay focused, don't look back and keep following Jesus.

THEIR TESTIMONY IS FOR YOU TOO

Romans 4:20-25 NKJV

[20] He did not waver at the promise of God through unbelief, but was strengthened in faith, giving glory to God, [21] and being fully convinced that what He had promised He was also able to perform. [22] And therefore "it was accounted to him for righteousness."

[23] Now it was not written for his sake alone that it was imputed to him, [24] but also for us. It shall be imputed to us who believe in Him who raised up Jesus our Lord from the dead, [25] who was delivered up because of our offenses, and was raised because of our justification.

Abraham being counted as righteous was recorded, not just for his benefit but for our benefit too. Why? God loves to keep record of His goodness, His works and His miracles. Those things that are revealed are for us, our children and the generations to come. We have to know that what God did for Abraham, He will also do for us. In the same manner, when we hear someone's testimony, it is a record for their benefit and for ours too—however, we can't waver at God's promises through doubt or unbelief.

Let me drive this home a little further because I really want you to get this.

When I was reading an email celebrating the newest book of a tremendously gifted prophet, I got hit with that woe is me feeling and in my heart, I thought, "Well that sure is good for her, but what about me!" I instantly felt bad and repented, but I also knew it was a wonderful example to include in the very book I was writing, the book you hold in your hands. Being one who likes to get straight to the meat, I normally don't read all of the reviews and endorsements. However, on this occasion, out of all the reviews that were written about the book, I decided to read one that said how wonderful it is for this prophet to enter heaven and be able to see. What's better is that she has a commission from God to help others to step in.

This is a great example of unrighteous indignation. After I read her testimony and the endorsement, I literally felt, "Well...that must be nice! It's wonderful that she enters Heaven and has all of these experiences"—feeling really slighted and bothered. What usually happens is that we stop there and we allow it to go downhill instead of uphill.

I took a moment to collect myself—to pray and repent. It was then I went on to read the second sentence of the endorsement. The first sentence was "just" what I felt, "It's wonderful that she enters Heaven and has all of these experiences!" The statement from the endorser was one of praise and excitement for what God was doing, but my statement held feelings of unrighteous indignation, bitterness and rejection.

I think that is amazing! The endorser and I said the exact same thing, but the spirit behind it was different. As the endorsement continued, it was stated how what was better than the individual giftedness was the invitation extended to us all as a result. Voila! That's exactly what I felt "after" feeling sorry for myself and then repenting. It was so comforting to read because it felt like God was confirming exactly what He was saying to me.

Oftentimes, we get caught up with the "individual" and miss the "invitation."

Don't miss it! God is willing to do it again...with you, for you and through you.

We have to remember not to forget to give God the glory and the praise for what He is doing in the lives of our brothers and sisters. He is using each and every one of us to profit the body of Christ. The manifestation of the Spirit is given to each one to profit withal. Others being used by God is going to profit all of us. When our sisters are doing their work and it is bringing God glory, we have to be careful to give God the praise and honor for what He is doing in their lives and make sure we don't take or hold back His glory because we want to be jealous. So just as it profits the body of Christ when God uses them, it profits the body of Christ when God uses you.

So don't stop at unrighteous indignation, if you've experienced it. Try to see the good part about it. Try to see how it is benefiting the body of Christ at large and that will help you to give God praise. You might initially feel, "Well, oh nice for her, but woe is me." How common and easy it is to fall into "woe is me," but try to reframe your thinking into how it is benefiting the body of Christ and you personally. Then thank God and praise Him for it.

Before you fall into the trap of jealousy, tell yourself, "Wait, this is a testimony of God's goodness and I can rest assured He will do the same for me!" Put your eyes back on God's goodness and His faithfulness and take them off of the person. Don't let your peace be stolen—for if you have no peace, you can be sure you are lacking in faith.

UNRIGHTEOUS INDIGNATION

We must be careful about falling into unrighteousness indignation. When we hear other people's testimony and we have this unrighteous indignation that rises within us and says, "Well...that must be nice!" We say this with the attitude that yes of course it would happen for "her," of course it would happen for "him" and we kind of, in that moment, forget about all the times and all the things that God has already done for "us." We really have to think, "Did I press in the way I needed to when He revealed this to me, when He showed this to me, when I had that experience—did I press in like I should have, did I pursue it like I should have, did I run after it with all that is within me?" We have to be careful not to discredit what God has shown us or what He has done for us.

Oftentimes we discredit and discount our experiences and magnify other people's experiences as better or greater than our own and then we look as if we were slighted. On the other hand, we also can feel a sense of entitlement too. But we have to make sure we value what God is doing in our lives and that we are good stewards over the revelation and the experiences He is bringing and calling us into. We have to make sure we are pressing in and getting all that He wants us to get and being good stewards over the little—not despising the little. Those who are good stewards over the small things are the ones who receive much.

So, when you hear about the testimony of others, just know that they may have stewarded the small things well. God is not a respecter of persons. He loves us just as much and He'll do the same things for us. He wants the same intimate relationship with us all. So, I would beseech you to press in, to pursue with all of your heart, to abandon anything that would get in the way of your pursuit of godliness and getting into His presence to behold His beauty and inquire in His temple. He will show you His beauty and He will answer when you come and inquire.

I would encourage you to press in, press in, press in! Press in to receive the big, the nuggets that you are looking for, that you are believing for, that you are hoping for, that you desire in your heart. Be a good steward over the small things and everything else will follow. Seek first the Kingdom of God and His righteousness and all these things will be added unto you (Matthew 6:33).

It may seem odd; however, it is quite common that many have found themselves jealous of another person's relationship with God.

When Miriam and Aaron criticized Moses, God showed up for him. It wasn't to show Miriam that she wasn't as special or as loved, but to point out the faithfulness and humility that Moses possessed and that God honored. The Bible says that Moses was very humble—more humble than any other person on earth (Numbers 12:3 NLT). Why wouldn't God honor him? Moses was humble and faithful, which caused God to trust him and speak to him differently than anyone else—face-to-face.

God will honor any of His children who are faithful and humble. When it was time for Moses to pass on, guess what—God was with Joshua, just as He was with Moses. We have to understand the times and seasons and what God is accomplishing through those He has appointed.

Always know it is the work and the will of the Lord that matters. Paul had to correct the people for their preferential attitudes concerning him and Barnabas. He pointed out that they just plant and water, but it is God alone who gives the increase.

There was no need for jealousy between Paul and Peter, both apostles, one called to the Jews and the other to the Gentiles. It was evident that both were called and chosen by God, none better than the other.

ADJUST YOUR VISION

You have to make sure that your vision is adjusted, focused and refined. When you behold or see someone else's light shining brightly, you want to be sure you're not blinded by jealousy. We have to have the right viewpoint. However, instead of having the right viewpoint, a Godly viewpoint, many have become blinded and unable to see that the brightness of the rising of others is also a brightness that God wants you to carry as well.

Don't get discouraged. The reason it is written, "Let your light shine so that men would see your good works and glorify my Father in Heaven," is because it was always designed for God to get the glory out of us shining brightly, out of us letting our light shine. It was never created for us to see someone else's light shining and then we, instead of looking at God, look inwardly to ourselves and determine within ourselves that we are not good enough. Instead of turning to God and glorifying Him, we look to ourselves and become abased and in that position we're not able to go to God with grateful hearts and with thankfulness. Instead we begin to murmur and complain because we have failed to see that which we have beheld is what God wants to do in our lives as well.

We have to be careful not to make idols out of other people's success and not to make idols out of other people's greatness. I say this because when you look at someone and you see them succeeding, prospering, and being great, you become jealous instead of glorifying your Father in Heaven. You look at them, exalt their greatness and fail to realize that it's God's glory. It's the Spirit of God working in them and through them and that same Spirit that is working in them and through them, is the same Spirit dwelling in you.

Don't choose to focus on their greatness and not on the God who created that greatness. When you have a focus on greatness and not on the God of greatness, your focus and your viewpoint become distorted and it could possibly lead to destruction and discouragement. Greatness without God—greatness outside of God is not a good thing. When you can look at someone's greatness and recognize that it is God, you are able to step into it, tap into it, behold it, grab hold of it and see the same miracle working power that is at work in their lives at work in your own as well.

HIS RULING PEACE

We know that in all things we overcome by the blood of the Lamb and by the word of our testimony. That's why we have the privilege of being peace-makers. God made it easy for us to be peace-makers by giving us His peace and leaving it with us. He doesn't give as the world gives and thus, we don't have to receive what the world would offer us. We don't have to conform or behave like those of the world because we are simply different. We are a peculiar people. The world may look and see what you are going through and think it's strange for you to have peace, but for us it's the norm—it's expected—it's the Kingdom. It is our birthright to have peace in our minds and hearts. We need His peace to rule in our hearts. Let His peace be a guard for your heart, your mind, your thoughts and your emotions.

TO SHINE OR TO BE SHAMED

Psalm 34:5 CEV
Keep your eyes on the LORD!
You will shine like the sun

and never blush with shame.

The Bible says that those who look to Jesus are radiant! Their faces are never covered with shame. NEVER!

So, I encourage you—KEEP YOUR EYES ON THE LORD!

FINAL WORD

Overcomer you have reached the end!

I want to thank you for taking the time and finding the courage to read this book. Thank you for the part you play in the transformation taking place in the body of Christ.

Thank you for the contributions you have made, the prayers you have prayed and the support you have shown to your sisters.

I salute you as you move forward with a new level of grace, mercy, and love.

I bless you in the name of Jesus Christ, our Lord and Savior.

I declare the blessings of God over you and your relationships. Go forward and prosper!

In Christ,
Floydise Paquette

ABOUT THE AUTHOR

Floydise Paquette is a beloved daughter of God through His Son, Jesus Christ, a mother, author, and entrepreneur. She has a heart on fire to see the Kingdom of Heaven advanced and the Family of God united and moving together in love. She is called to the daughters of God with a unique voice and powerful mandate to encourage, strengthen, and build. God is using her gift of writing to bring healing and restoration to the hearts of His people. Visit us on our website: www.overcomingjealousy.com or www.floydisepaquette.com

REFERENCES

Chapter 1
1. https://www.merriam-webster.com/dictionary/jealous
2. https://www.merriam-webster.com/dictionary/jealousy
3. 3 https://www.dictionary.com/browse/jealous
4. https://www.google.com/search?safe=active&source=hp&ei=KMPpXPOBKdGe_QajiKF4&q=jealous&oq=jealous&gs_l=psy-ab.12..0l10.3514.4529..4708...1.0..0.176.866.3j5......0....1..gws-wiz.....6..35i39j0i131.mG4Loh5sD94

Chapter 2
5. https://www.merriam-webster.com/dictionary/jealousy
6. https://www.merriam-webster.com/dictionary/compete
7. https://www.merriam-webster.com/dictionary/covetous
8. https://en.wikipedia.org/wiki/Envy

Chapter 4
9. https://www.bing.com/search?q=inferiority+complex&qs=LS&pq=inferiority+com&sc=8-15&cvid=8C

86EAC51B5245E187003F324973A39F&FORM=Q
BLH&sp=1&ghc=1

10. https://www.merriam-webster.com/dictionary/
inferiority%20complex

11. https://www.merriam-webster.com/thesaurus/
bitterness

Chapter 6

12. New Testament Greek lexicon entry 1922. The New
Strong's Exhaustive Concordance of the Bible by
James Strong, LL.D., S.T.D., Published © 2010 by
Thomas Nelson Publishers. All rights reserved.

Index

A

abomination, 97
affirmation, 76, 202–3
agreement, 6, 19, 59, 61, 73, 97, 100, 106, 113, 135, 202
anger, 3–4, 11, 25–26, 31, 49, 64–65, 87, 117
anointing, 33, 38, 42, 56, 87, 104
arguments, 24, 47, 165–66, 204
armor, 98, 151, 167, 172, 175
attitude, 2–3, 8–9, 46, 62, 64, 80, 82, 89, 91, 125–26, 210
authority, 6, 57, 81, 110, 114–15, 153

B

bait, 127–29, 131, 133, 135, 137
battle, 112, 132, 142, 168–70, 177, 179, 186, 192
bitterness, 31, 47, 77, 87, 100, 116–17, 209
blessings, 16, 20, 30–31, 54, 56, 61, 74–75, 77, 92, 131, 135–36, 145, 159, 165, 168
brightness, 213

C

Made in the USA
San Bernardino, CA
27 January 2020

63658272R00149